O say can you see ~~through~~ by the dawn's early l[ight]
what so proudly we hail'd at the twilight's last gleam[ing]
[W]hose broad stripes & bright stars through the perilous fig[ht]
['e]r the ramparts we watch'd, were so gallantly strea[ming]
      And the rocket's red glare, the bomb bursting in [air]
      Gave proof through the night that our flag was still [there]
O say does that star-spangled banner yet wave
O'er the land of the free & the home of the brave?

On the shore dimly seen through the mists of the [deep]
    Where the foe's haughty host in dread silence re[poses]
[W]hat is that which the breeze, o'er the towering stee[p]
As it fitfully blows, half conceals, half discloses?
      Now it catches the gleam of the morning's first be[am]
      In full glory reflected now shines in the strea[m]
'Tis the star-spangled banner — O long may it wa[ve]
O'er the land of the free & the home of the bra[ve]

And where is that band who so vauntingly swo[re]
That the havoc of war & the battle's confusion
A home & a Country should leave us no more?
— ~~The~~ ~~~~
      Their blood has wash'd out their foul footstep's [pollution]
No refuge could save the hireling & slave
From the terror of flight or the gloom of the gra[ve]
And the star-spangled banner in triumph doth wa[ve]
O'er the land of the free & the home of the bra[ve]

O thus be it ever when freemen shall stand
Between their lov'd home & the war's desolation;
Blest with vict'ry & peace may the heav'n rescued l[and]
Praise the power that hath made & preserv'd us a n[ation]
      Then conquer we must when our cause it is ju[st]
      And this be our motto — "In God is our trust,"
And the star-spangled banner in triumph shall wave

STAR-SPANGLED

The Story of a Flag, a Battle, and the American Anthem

by

TIM GROVE

ABRAMS BOOKS FOR YOUNG READERS
NEW YORK

Cataloging-in-Publication Data has been applied for
and may be obtained from the Library of Congress.

ISBN 978-1-4197-4102-9

Text copyright © 2020 Tim Grove
Edited by Howard W. Reeves
Book design by Melissa Jane Barrett

Endpapers are photographs of Francis Scott Key's original draft of the
poem that inspired America's national anthem; courtesy of the Library
of Congress. The decorative elements on the title page and chapter
openers were created using various period graphic ornaments.

Printed and bound in China
10 9 8 7 6 5 4 3 2 1

Abrams Books for Young Readers are available at special
discounts when purchased in quantity for premiums and
promotions as well as fundraising or educational use. Special
editions can also be created to specification. For details,
contact specialsales@abramsbooks.com or the address below.

Abrams® is a registered trademark of Harry N. Abrams, Inc.

ABRAMS The Art of Books
195 Broadway, New York, NY 10007
abramsbooks.com

★ CONTENTS ★

List of
✴ CHARACTERS ✴

AMERICAN

MAJOR GEORGE ARMISTEAD
the commander of Fort McHenry

DR. WILLIAM BEANES
a physician and leading resident of
Upper Marlboro, Maryland

THOMAS KEMP
a ship builder and shipyard owner in
Fells Point, Baltimore

FRANCIS (FRANK) SCOTT KEY
a lawyer from Georgetown

MARY PICKERSGILL
a Baltimore business woman

JOHN SKINNER
a prisoner exchange agent

**MAJOR GENERAL
SAMUEL SMITH**
a Maryland senator and lifelong
Baltimore citizen in charge of the
defense of Baltimore

**BRIGADIER GENERAL
JOHN STRICKER**
the leader in charge of the American
army at North Point

BRITISH

**MIDSHIPMAN
ROBERT BARRETT**
a fifteen-year-old sailor

COLONEL ARTHUR BROOKE
General Ross's second in command

**VICE ADMIRAL SIR
ALEXANDER COCHRANE ****
the top British military leader in the
Chesapeake Bay

**REAR ADMIRAL SIR
GEORGE COCKBURN ****
the second in command of the British
naval forces in the Chesapeake Bay
(after Cochrane arrived)

**LIEUTENANT GEORGE
ROBERT GLEIG**
an eighteen-year-old Scottish soldier

**MAJOR GENERAL GEORGE
ROBERT ROSS**
the British army commander in charge
of land forces

** These two British admirals—
Cochrane and Cockburn have similar
names. Because it is nonfiction, the
names can't be altered, so pay special
attention to keep the characters apart.

★ PREFACE ★

EVERYTHING THAT HAPPENS IN THIS BOOK IS true, and all the characters were real people. The book is based on historical evidence. Historians try to put a puzzle together from the many pieces of historical evidence they find while doing research. Sometimes there are questions and holes in the story for which the evidence doesn't provide answers. What did Thomas Kemp look like? No portrait or description exists. Or, where were he and Mary Pickersgill during the Battle of Baltimore? They didn't leave a record of their activity, or if they did, the record has been lost. What did the former slaves who fought for the Americans think? What did the formerly enslaved people who sided with the British think? Most enslaved people were not taught to read and write, so few written records provide this kind of information. Charles Ball is an exception, and I wanted to include his story because he provides a first-person perspective.

I chose to tell this story from different perspectives because all history events can be viewed from more than one angle. At times, historical evidence contradicts itself and historical witnesses offer different versions of the story. When there is a contradiction, historians must weigh the validity of each source and decide which evidence is stronger or which voices to include. Every person and event in the past is complex and layered and worth looking at from multiple directions. That's why history is so fascinating! I have attempted to show you some of the questions that historians ask and to provide a glimpse into the detective work that I think makes researching the past so fun. Be sure to read the Notes section for additional information.

✯ INTRODUCTION ✯

YOU KNOW THE NATIONAL ANTHEM. "O! Say, can you see?" I bet you could hum it right now. You've probably sung it at a sporting event, or during the beginning of a concert. Maybe you've watched the Olympics and heard the anthem play when an American wins gold. Most, if not all, countries have a national anthem—a song that represents them. Many anthems have words: Some proclaim values such as courage and loyalty that describe the country's citizens. France's popular anthem, "La Marseillaise," is a call for citizens to fight for freedom against oppression. The British anthem is a prayer for the health of the reigning king or queen. Anthems inspire patriotism and pride in one's country. The United States of America's anthem, unlike most, tells the story of a historic event. While many Americans know the words, they don't all know the story. This book tells that story through the eyes of people who lived it, including Mary Pickersgill, Thomas Kemp, George Cockburn, Francis Scott Key, Samuel Smith, and Alexander Cochrane. They lived very different lives, yet their stories would become woven together into one grand narrative. At the center of the story is a flag that would one day be called the Star-Spangled Banner. Many years ago it flew over a fort in the city of Baltimore during a battle with Great Britain.

The Battle of Baltimore was one of many battles during the War of 1812, a confusing name because although the war began that year, it lasted until 1815. During the war, fighting took place in various parts of the North American continent, mostly in four main areas: along the Canada–United States border and into southern Canada, at spots along America's western boundary, in the Chesapeake Bay region, and along the Gulf Coast in the South.

MIRROR-OFFICE, June 22, 1812.

WAR DECLARED!!

Extract of a Letter from Washington, received in this City,
dated June 18, 1812.

" The injunction of secrecy is just removed. An act
has passed, and been approved by the President, declaring
—THAT WAR EXISTS BETWEEN THE KINGDOM OF
GREAT-BRITAIN AND IRELAND AND THEIR DEPEN-
DENCIES, AND THE UNITED STATES OF AMERI-
CA ; *and also authorizing the President to employ the land
and naval force to carry it on, and to issue Letters of
Marque and Reprisal.*"

In the House of Representatives—Yeas 79, Nays 49, majority for
War 30; Senate—Yeas 19, Noes 13, majority 6.

From the New-York Evening Post of Saturday last.

Brigadier-General BLOOMFIELD, commander of the United States' forces
on this station, received a letter by a government Express from the Secretary at War, this morning, and immediately issued the following :—

(copy)

" GENERAL ORDERS.

" HEAD-QUARTERS, 20th June, 1812.
" General Bloomfield announces to the troops that " WAR IS DECLAR-
ED BY THE UNITED STATES AGAINST GREAT-BRITAIN."
" BY ORDER,

" R. H. MACPHERSON, Aid-de-Camp."

Government Expresses passed through this city, about 10 o'clock for
Albany and Boston, with the above intelligence.

A news bulletin in the form of a poster called a broadside announced the
declaration of war against Great Britain, June 22, 1812.

Although today Americans and Canadians view it as a separate war, British people often consider the War of 1812 part of a larger conflict the United Kingdom and other European countries fought against France. That's if they think of it at all, because in British history the War of 1812 does not hold much importance. In North American history, the war is important because it confirmed the United States of America's independence from Great Britain. It was a key event in ensuring Canadian freedom as well, from the United States. Canada was not yet its own country, but was made up of separate colonies that were part of the British Empire. Some politicians in the United States wanted to expand American territory by capturing parts of Canada.

The War of 1812 was the first war declared by the new United States. America was a baby among powerful countries such as France, Great Britain, Russia, Austria, and Prussia (later Germany). Its very existence was fragile, and President James Madison's declaration of war against Britain was a bold move that only some Americans agreed with. But those who wanted war were fed up with Britain's disregard for America's freedom to trade with other European countries and its kidnapping (called impressment) of American sailors from American ships to work on its fleet. Britain thought it could push America around. And to a degree it could. Great Britain's powerful navy ruled the seas; America barely owned a navy. The events that played out on the water around Baltimore would have a large impact on American history.

CHAPTER

1

A SITTING DUCK

Early September 1814

Located along the Patapsco River at the top of the Chesapeake Bay in Maryland, Baltimore waited. With its bustling harbor and famous shipyards, America's third-largest city of fifty thousand inhabitants was a juicy target for the mighty armada of more than fifty British navy ships sailing toward it. Earlier that year an English newspaper had called Baltimore a nest of pirates. Another paper had written: "There is not a spot in the whole United States where an infliction of Britain's vengeance [revenge] will be more entitled to our applause than . . . Baltimore."

In August, the British military had stormed into America's young capital city, Washington, D.C., forty miles southwest of Baltimore. They seized an opportunity to demonstrate their power by burning important government buildings in the weakly guarded city. The American troops, mostly inexperienced militia called up at the last minute, embarrassed themselves with a half-hearted attempt to stop them. Their fearful run from the enemy was dubbed "the Bladensburg Races," referring to the town outside Washington where the encounter occurred. The British set fire to the Capitol, the navy yard, and the president's White House. Only the exterior walls of the dwelling survived (along with a famous portrait of President George Washington, which

The British set the White House on fire during their invasion of Washington, D.C., August 24, 1814. This image is from a book published in 1816.

had been hauled to safety). James Madison, the fourth president, and his wife, Dolley, had fled earlier in the day.

From their rooftops, the citizens of Baltimore stared in horror at the fiery glow on the horizon. The British military was a seemingly unstoppable force.

The inhabitants of Baltimore knew they were in the bull's-eye next. They had mixed feelings. They also had strong feelings. One of Baltimore's nicknames was "Mobtown." Throughout history, the citizens of Baltimore had never needed much excuse to form an angry mob and riot. In 1812, Baltimore was home to a large population of French, Irish, and German immigrants who did not like the British. They thought anyone who supported Britain was disloyal to the United States. When President Madison declared war against Britain in June that year, a Baltimore newspaper pub-

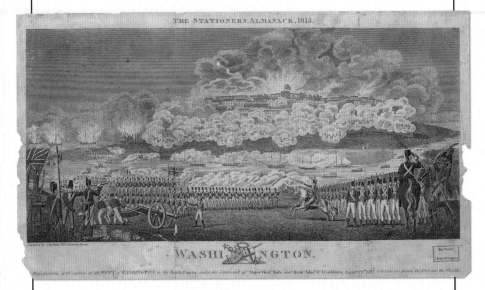

This engraving appeared in a British publication, the *Stationer's Almanack*, in 1815. While its title says it depicts the British capture of Washington, D.C., the British only attacked the city and burned some of the main public buildings.

lisher named Alexander Hanson printed articles opposing the war and praising Britain. This of course did not sit well with many people in Baltimore. An angry mob armed with hooks, axes, and other weapons destroyed Hanson's offices and printing press and beat him and his supporters. Sadly, the first few deaths of the war occurred not on a battlefield but on the streets of Baltimore.

When the United States declared war, the British military was already occupied with a long war against France and their primary focus was on Europe. That left Britain's Canadian territory poorly defended. The United States took advantage of this and in July invaded Canada, forcing the British to defend their territory with the few troops that were there, plus forces of the Canadian militia (including some French-speaking Canadians) and Indian allies. A series of skirmishes and battles followed.

★ ★ ★ ★ ★ ★

Map of

NORTH
AMERICA

War of 1812
in North America

★ ★ ★ ★ ★ ★

MAP KEY	
 British blockade	
● Major battle	0 150
◯ Area of fighting	MILES

British North America
(Canada)

Territory of Massachusetts

Michigan Territory

New York

Vermont

New Hampshire

Massachusetts

Rhode Island

Connecticut

Pennsylvania

New Jersey

Indiana Territory

Ohio

Illinois Territory

Delaware

Maryland

Virginia

Kentucky

Tennessee

North Carolina

South Carolina

Mississippi Territory

Georgia

Spanish Territory

Louisiana

Florida

N

America's fourth president, James Madison, engraved by David Edwin, sometime during his term between 1809 and 1817.

Despite their lack of focus, the British defeated American troops near Detroit and Queenston. In the Great Lakes region, the Battle of Lake Erie was an American victory, as were the Battle of the Thames (River) in western Ontario and the Battle of York in present-day Toronto.

At sea, when war began, the British navy numbered just over eighty vessels in North American waters, with around twenty devoted to a blockade (the others were involved in military protection). The Navy attempted to stop American merchant shipping traffic by blockading major port cities on the East Coast of the United States starting in the middle states and gradually expanding north to include New England and south to Savannah, Georgia, as the war progressed and more British ships became available. By the end of 1812, the British had begun blockading traffic moving into the Atlantic Ocean from the Chesapeake Bay. This directly impacted Baltimore. The British Navy maintained a presence in the Chesapeake Bay starting in March 1813 when it began raiding various towns on the bay, including one near Baltimore.

In May 1814, news arrived on American shores that the French leader Napoleon Bonaparte had surrendered, Britain's war with France was over, and its military could turn its full attention on the Americans. This was not good news! On June 26, President Madison's sources began sending warnings. His diplomats in London wrote that a large number of British troops would in fact be heading toward America soon. Confirmation came with London newspapers reporting in mid-July that British troops were boarding ships bound for America. Where would they appear?

For the citizens of Baltimore, the war so far had not been too bad. Most of the military action had been far away. But life was about to get more challenging for the Americans living in the Chesapeake Bay region.

The British were winning the war. If Baltimore fell, American independence might be at stake. The freedom that was earned at such a high cost during the American Revolution could be lost. Baltimore had to stand firm.

View of Baltimore from Federal Hill. While Edward Weber drew this image about
thirty years after the battle, its depiction of a harbor full of ships is accurate to
1814—even the steamboat. Steamboats began regularly scheduled service on the
Chesapeake Bay in 1813.

CHAPTER

2

A SUITABLE ENSIGN–1813

Mary Pickersgill, thirty-eight, ran a thriving sewing business from her two-and-a-half story home on Albemarle Street a few blocks from Baltimore's harbor. In 1813, not many women owned and operated a business, but Mary's husband had died and she had a thirteen-year-old daughter, Caroline, to care for. Her mother, Rebecca Young, also a widow, lived with her, as did three nieces, a free black girl named Grace,

This daguerreotype (early photograph) is the only known photo of Mary Pickersgill. It was taken in 1850, many years after the Battle of Baltimore, when she was age seventy-four.

and an enslaved person (most likely female, name unknown). As if the small house wasn't crowded enough, Mary took in a male boarder who rented a room and took meals with the family. The boarder provided some extra income.

Fortunately, the nieces were all old enough to contribute to the sewing work, as was Grace, who was an indentured servant hired for six years to learn the sewing trade in exchange for room and board. Her indenture agreement stated she would work alongside Mary to learn "the art and mystery of housework and plain sewing." Mary and her mother specialized in sewing flags, commonly called colors. She advertised her business in Baltimore

Mary's two-and-a-half-story brick house was surrounded by a bustling neighborhood with many small businesses supporting the maritime industry.

newspapers. One advertisement read: "The Military Gentlemen of Baltimore are respectfully informed that they can be supplied with Silk Standards & Cavalry Colors, and other Colors of every description, finished in compleat [sic] order. Also, Colors for the Navy, on the most reasonable terms."

Pickersgill came from a family of flag makers loyal to the patriot cause during the American Revolution. She shared a birth year with the United States, born in Philadelphia in 1776, five months before the Declaration of Independence was signed. Her father, William Young, a goldsmith, was active in patriot circles and believed that the colonies should be free. To the British he was the enemy, so when the British army occupied Philadelphia during the Revolution, the family fled west to Lebanon, Pennsylvania. Mary's uncle, Benjamin Flower, also a patriot, oversaw the removal of army supplies and munitions out of Philadelphia. He was also responsible for moving the Liberty Bell to a safe location.

William left the family to continue helping the war effort. In Allentown, Pennsylvania, he contracted camp fever, a disease that brought high body temperature, delirium, and often death. A notation in the Young family bible indicates that he died from camp fever only five months after the family fled Philadelphia. With six children and Mary just a baby, Rebecca Young must have felt overwhelmed with questions of how the family would make ends meet. When the British evacuated Philadelphia, she moved her family back to the city to live with her brother's family on Walnut Street. Rebecca began to produce supplies for the

The most famous flag maker in American history is Betsy Ross, a Philadelphia woman who was sewing flags at the same time as Mary's mother, Rebecca. Legend says General George Washington visited Betsy's shop and requested the first flag, but no historical evidence confirms this story. The descendants of Rebecca Young asserted that she made the first flag of the Revolution for General Washington, the Grand Union flag raised over Washington's Cambridge, Massachusetts, headquarters in 1776. But no evidence confirms this story either. The two women, business rivals, undoubtedly knew each other given the small community of flag makers in the city. One known source lists them both but it doesn't relate to flags. A January 1779 ledger listing supply producers includes Rebecca Young on one page and Betsy on the opposite page. (She's listed as Elizabeth Ashburn, her new name after she remarried following husband John Ross's death). Both made musket cartridges.

Philadelphia Packets, Mercantile line, agents Howell and
    Carpenter, 59 Smith's wharf

Phrow and Ready, tin plate workers, 69 Harrison street

Pickett George, carpenter, N. Eutaw street

Pickett John, merchant tailor, 242 Baltimore street

Pickering Jacob, cordwainer, Whiskey alley near Eutaw
    street

Pickersgill Mary, maker of ships colours, signals, &c. 60
    Albemarle street—*o t*

Pidgeon John, grocer, corner of Liberty and M'Elderry
    streets —*o t*

Pierce Elizabeth, widow, 34 Fell street—*f p*

Pierce John, innkeeper, 4 Market street—*f p*

Piet John and Co. hardware store, 246 Baltimore street

Pike Abraham, tobacconist, dwelling 26 N. Liberty street

Pike Henry and Co. hardware merchants, 21 S. Calvert
    street

Pilch James, grocer, County wharf—*f p*

Pilkington Thomas, tailor, 13 Fell street—*f p*

Pilgrim Nathaniel, plane maker, Franklin near Howard
    street—*w p*

Pindell John, coach maker, 29 Green street—*o t*

Pindell Richard, constable, 179 Bond street—*f p*

Pindle Charles R. 3 Liberty street—*o t*

Pinkney William, attorney and counsellor at law, 27 N.
    Gay street

Piper James, counting room head of Frederick street dock

Pise Louis, portrait painter and teacher of drawing, Vulcan
    alley

Pitts Thomas, cordwainer, Petticoat alley

Pitt William, dry good store, 16 W. Allisanna street—*f p*

Pitt Richard, sea captain, Wilk between Ann and Wolfe
    streets

Plane George, cabinet maker, 14 Green street—*o t*

Placide Paul, cooper, Buchanan's wharf

Plasted Mary, widow, 3 Waggon alley

Pletenberg Christian, grocer, 70 High street—*o t*

Pleasants John P. commission merchant, 8 Light street
    wharf, dwelling Pleasant street—*w p*

Plimton James, sea captain, Wolfe near Allisanna st.—*f p*

The Baltimore City Directory lists Mary as a "maker of ships colours."
The "ot" means the Old Town neighborhood; "fp" means Fells Point.

Continental Army. She first made musket cartridges, then began sewing blankets, drum covers, linings for caps, and later, flags.

In 1781, Rebecca Young placed an ad in the *Pennsylvania Packet* newspaper advertising "all kinds of Colours [flags] for the army and navy, made and sold on the most reasonable terms." She was one of only a few people to advertise a flag-making business at the time. Records show that she sewed six flags for the Continental Army in 1781 and 1782.

After the American Revolution ended in 1783, two of Mary's siblings settled in Baltimore. Her sister married the son of a shipyard owner. Mary and her mother began spending time in the Maryland city. At some point, Mary met an English merchant named John Pickersgill, whom she married in 1795 at age nineteen. The couple moved to Philadelphia and began a family. Of the four daughters born in the next four years, only Caroline lived. Business took John to England, where he died suddenly in 1805. Mary was now a widow, just like her mother. The following year, she and Caroline moved to Baltimore to live near family.

Pickersgill's shop was surrounded by potential customers because it sat in the middle of a lively neighborhood filled with people who worked for the maritime industry. Just down the block lived one of the most famous sea captains, Thomas Boyle. A few streets over sat the shipyards that built the famed Baltimore schooners, the fastest ships on the waves. Sailing vessels carried two types of flags: signal flags used to communicate with other ships while at sea, and merchant flags to identify their owners. A large schooner could use dozens of different signal flags. When arriving in a foreign port, a ship would usually display its country's colors and the port country's colors.

The other enterprise that used flags was the military. Most

616

Pickersgill's shop catered to both the military and the maritime industries. Ships of every size used colorful signal flags to communicate messages.

of its flags identified regiments, militias, and other military units. Because America was at war with Great Britain, there was an even greater need for flags should actual combat occur. Since March 1813, the British navy had been sailing around the Chesapeake Bay, disrupting commerce and threatening to cause damage. While battles had so far mostly occurred near the Canadian border, the citizens of Baltimore lived with dread that the British might suddenly arrive on their doorstep.

Fortunately, Fort McHenry gave them protection. The star-shaped brick structure sat at the tip of a long spit of land and guarded the entrance to the Baltimore harbor. It was the perfect location for a fort. Although Fort McHenry had been standing for thirteen years, it lacked a flag. The fort's commander, Major George Armistead, wrote to General Samuel Smith: "We, Sir, are ready at Fort McHenry to defend Baltimore against invading by the enemy. That is to say, we are ready except we have no suitable ensign to display over the fort, and it is my desire to have a flag so large that the British will have no difficulty in seeing it from a distance." One would think that a large flag would draw unwanted enemy attention, but it was standard procedure to fly flags over forts. Prior to arriving at his command in Baltimore, Armistead had served at Fort Niagara in northern New York. There, he had flown a large flag over the fort.

The design Mary followed was the second official version of the United States flag. The Flag Act of 1795 signed by President George Washington designated a fifteen-star-and-fifteen-stripe flag, based on the number of states at that time. Vermont and Kentucky were the first two states added after the original thirteen. Although by 1813 there were eighteen states, not until 1818 did a law designate the familiar design we see today where the stripes represent the original states and the stars represent the current number of states.

BALTIMORE

PORT

ET

RADE

FERRY

BRANCHE

Ch. S.
White Marsh

Ferry

Ferry

P A T A P

P

2 ½

2 ½

2 ½

2

2 ½

1 ½

2

This French map of Baltimore shows Fort McHenry at the end of a long peninsula. Look for the star.

On a warm day in June of 1813, several men stopped by Pickersgill's business to place an order. They entered the small front room where Mary and Rebecca displayed samples of their work. They may have seen her ad in the newspaper or knew of her excellent work. Acting on behalf of Major Armistead, they asked Mary if she would be willing to make two large flags for the fort: one 30-by-42-foot flag (about one-fourth the size of a modern basketball court; 9.14 by 12.80 m) and a smaller 17-by-25-foot flag (5.18 x 7.62 m). The larger one, called a garrison flag, would be flown in good weather, the smaller one, called a storm flag, would fly in bad weather and during military action.

Mary faced two big challenges if she agreed to the job. First, she had never made a flag so large. How complicated would it be? Would she have space in her small home to spread it out? And what about materials? Would she be able to secure all she needed to complete the order? Second, they wanted the flags in six weeks! She had other projects under way. The military feared the British could attack Baltimore soon and the fort needed a flag. The project would require Mary to enlist the help of everyone in her household who could sew. They would need to work long hours, late into the night. The flags would be stitched by hand. (The sewing machine had not yet been invented. Elias Howe received the first American patent for a sewing machine in 1846.)

A savvy businesswoman, Pickersgill agreed to the order and embarked on a project that produced what is today one of America's national treasures. She would need yards of bunting, loosely woven wool fabric which was perfect for flags; strong yet pliable and easy to sew. Ironically, bunting was made only in

Sudbury, England! Despite the British navy's best attempt at a blockade, ships bringing supplies managed to slip through. She needed red, white, and blue bunting for fifteen stripes and the canton (the blue top inner corner). She would use cotton material for the white stars.

Once her supplies were in place, Mary would have had to decide on her process. This meant doing what she could to minimize the amount of material. Imported material was costly and she needed a lot of it. On the large flag, the stripes would be 2 feet (61 cm) wide! Bunting came in 18-inch- (45.7 cm) wide bolts. So, she ended up cutting some strips in thirds and attaching 6-inch (15 cm) strips to create the stripes. Historians don't know where she purchased her cotton material, perhaps at one of several textile warehouses in Baltimore. In any case it was also expensive, so she wouldn't want to end up having to sew thirty stars per flag (fifteen for each side). Plus, each star on the large flag was 2 feet (61 cm) wide from tip to tip. She ended up using a method called reverse appliqué. She sewed all fifteen stars on the blue canton, then turned it over and carefully cut the blue fabric behind each star, revealing the white star underneath.

Mary didn't record the order in which she sewed the two flags. A letter that her daughter, Caroline, wrote many years later revealed how Mary solved the space issue: "The flag being so very large, my mother was obliged to obtain permission from the proprietors of [Brown's brewery] which was in our neighborhood, to spread it out in their malthouse." Caroline also wrote that her mother "worked many nights until midnight in order to complete the job in the given time." Since the light bulb had not yet been invented, Mary and her helpers relied

The original receipt for the two American flags ordered from Mary Pickersgill's shop for Fort McHenry.

as much as possible on natural light, but still needed to use candlelight or oil lamps after dark. No doubt the fine stitchwork required close lights, so there must have always been danger of fire near the fabric.

With the British navy lurking close by, Mary finished the last step in the process, which involved sewing a linen heading to the hoist side (side next to the pole) of the flag to allow it to be raised on the ninety-foot- (27.43 m) tall flag pole at Fort McHenry. Perhaps Mary hired a sailmaker, or maybe her brother John helped as he had the correct tools needed to push needles through the thick layers of material.

On August 19, soldiers came to collect the completed flags.

In typical government slowness, the government's commissary, Mr. James Calhoun, did not pay the bill until October 27. The receipt, which still exists today, indicates that the military paid $168.54 for the storm flag and $405.90 for the garrison flag for a grand total of $574.44 (about $8,800 today). The record is signed by Eliza Young. Historians have puzzled over whether Eliza was Mary's thirteen-year-old niece or her twenty-seven-year-old cousin.

No one knows exactly when Pickersgill's flags were first raised over Fort McHenry. But as the fort stood waiting the approaching British a year later, her stars and stripes waved above it in the wind.

CHAPTER

3

AMERICAN PRIZES

Why was Baltimore such an attractive target to the British? It had a large population but most important, it was a center of the ship-building industry and the ships it produced were causing financial damage to Britain's economy. Thomas Kemp owned one of the most successful shipyards in the city, not far from Mary Pickersgill's house. If the British attacked Baltimore, his business would most likely be in danger.

Kemp's shipyard stood at the corner of Washington and Allisanna Streets in the Fells Point neighborhood and produced sailing ships called schooners, famous for their speed and durability. Many of these ships were damaging British trade to the tune of millions of dollars. Called privateers, they were privately owned vessels permitted by the U.S. government to pursue and capture enemy shipping during war. They had received a government-issued document called a letter of marque and reprisal allowing them to capture British merchant ships. Without this commission, the sailors would be considered pirates. With it, their work was legal. Their crew's income came entirely from selling off the captured ships and their cargo. Big money awaited the owners of the fastest privateers.

Britain's navy may have ruled the waves, but it could not begin to protect all its merchant ships and other trade vessels on the seas around the world. Its blockade of America's coast couldn't stop American shipping either. In the dark of night Baltimore's privateers could make a run through the blockade. Baltimore had

a well-earned reputation as a center—if not *the* center—of the American privateering fleet. One hundred and twenty-six privateers were operated out of the city during the war, capturing over five hundred British ships and costing the English economy a fortune.

But the adventures were not just taking place on the high seas: American privateer crews were also active across the Atlantic Ocean, capturing ships in the enemy's waters. English newspapers declared outrage that "a horde of American cruisers should be allowed, unresisted and unmolested, to take, burn, or sink our own vessels in our own inlets and almost in sight of our own harbors."

Each week, Baltimore citizens could pick up the *Niles' Weekly Register* and find a list of privateers and their "American prizes," British ships that privateer crews had captured. The privateers Thomas Kemp built were usually on the list. Thomas had gained a national reputation because his yard had built the four most celebrated privateers in the country: the *Rossie*, the *Rolla*, the *Comet*,

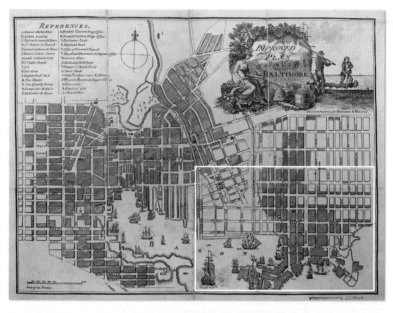

The Improved Plan of the City of Baltimore printed in 1804 by Warner and Hanna.

Detail from the Improved Plan showing the locations of Mary Pickersgill's shop (*left*) and Thomas Kemp's shipyard (*right*).

and the *Chasseur* (dubbed "the Pride of Baltimore"). Between the four ships, they seized prizes worth millions of dollars.

Though generally equipped with some guns, these schooner-type vessels were built to run, not fight. A privateer would stalk British ships on trade routes or lie in wait near hostile or neutral ports. Once an enemy ship was spotted, the chase began. When the ship was captured, the American captain would commandeer it and either sail it to a neutral port or to the United States, or confiscate the goods and sink it. The sailors on the captured ship were imprisoned and either exchanged or ransomed for money. To add to the challenge, not all captured ships were successfully

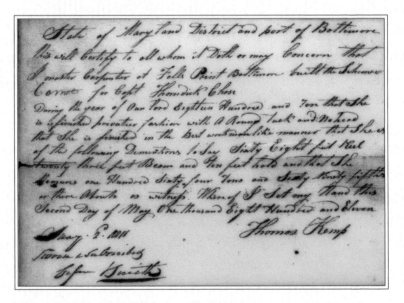

Every shipbuilder was required to create a title document, called a ship's certificate, at a ship's completion. It listed the name of the vessel, builder, owner, location of construction, and date of completion. It also included a description of the ship. In some ways, it acted like a birth certificate for the ship! This carpenter's certificate, signed by Thomas Kemp, verifies he built the *Comet* in 1810 for Captain Thorndick Chase.

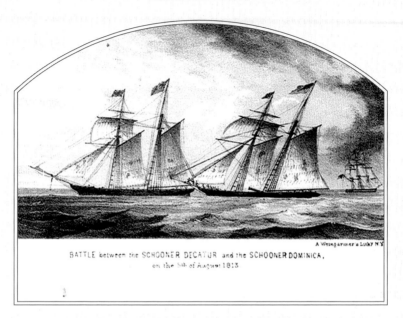

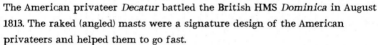

BATTLE between the SCHOONER DECATUR and the SCHOONER DOMINICA, on the 5th of August 1813

The American privateer *Decatur* battled the British HMS *Dominica* in August 1813. The raked (angled) masts were a signature design of the American privateers and helped them to go fast.

sent to port. Many of these prizes were recaptured by the British blockaders as they tried to enter U.S. ports.

What made the Baltimore privateers so successful? Thomas and other Baltimore shipbuilders were some of the most creative ship designers in America. They had figured out a unique design that allowed ships to move fast and maintain agility. No two ships were exactly alike. With each new ship, designers and builders attempted to find the right combination of design elements that made the ships faster and faster. Thomas had an office in his house near the shipyard where he labored over his plans. His special design increased speed by adding sails in top masts to catch the wind higher above the deck.

Though no two schooners were alike, they all had similar

Thomas Boyle became one of the most famous privateer captains. He lived in Fells Point.

elements. Shape contributed to effectiveness. The hull's V shape could easily cut through water. The schooners had what was called a sharp hull below the water that allowed them to sail closer to the wind (toward the direction from which the wind comes). The masts and stem and stern posts were raked, or angled, to further increase speed. To overcome water resistance, the ships had a large sail area

Aside from the sleek design, a key element to a Baltimore privateer's success was a skillful and daring captain. One of the most famous captains was Thomas Boyle, who lived around the corner from Mary Pickersgill. A native of Marblehead, Massachusetts, a town surrounded by water, Boyle went to sea at age ten and by sixteen was the sailing master of a ship, responsible for its navigation! At nineteen he moved to Baltimore, and with the success of the privateers under his control, he soon became famous. He commanded two ships built in the Kemp shipyard, the *Comet* and the *Chasseur*. When he returned to Baltimore from a daring voyage to England, the guns of Fort McHenry saluted him and crowds on Federal Hill cheered him.

with many topsails. Schooners made very efficient use of space for sails so they could capture as much wind as possible.

Building a ship was like putting a puzzle together and required men with many types of skills. (The work of shipbuilding was not considered safe or appropriate for women at this time.) Kemp's shipyard employed two dozen men, mostly carpenters and caulkers, people who sealed the cracks between boards and ensured the ship's seaworthiness. He also hired blacksmiths, riggers (who set all the ropes, wires, and chains controlling the sails and masts), and expert shipwrights (carpenters who work on ships). He needed to buy all kinds of supplies too, including timber, spars (wooden poles), beams, ironwork, copper spikes and rivets, rosin, and pitch. Surrounding the shipyards in Fells Point were many businesses, called chandleries, that sold supplies needed for the ships: block and tackle, pump, rope, and sails. In several nearby long, narrow buildings called ropewalks,

Baltimore schooners included a lot of sail area to catch as much wind as possible.

Thomas Kemp's shipyard would have been similar to the one in this engraving and would have employed about two dozen men, skilled at many different types of jobs.

men twisted hemp into the miles of rope needed to rig Baltimore's ships.

The most famous ship built at Fells Point was Kemp's masterpiece, the *Chasseur* (meaning "hunter" in French). It measured 116 feet long by 26 feet wide (35.35 x 7.92 m) and launched in December 1812. No contemporary picture of her exists, but Hezekiah Niles, editor of the *Niles' Weekly Register*, wrote at the time "she was indeed a fine specimen of naval architecture, and perhaps the most beautiful vessel that ever floated on the ocean. She sat as light and buoyant on the water as a graceful swan, and it required but very little imagination to feel that she was about to leave her watery element, and fly into the clear, blue sky."

An astute businessman, Kemp often bought shares of ownership in the privateers his yard built. Many shipbuilders did this as an investment and to help ensure future repair contracts. Privateers usually earned pure profit after one or two voyages. Their owners could make a lot of money from the sale of prizes (the captured ships and goods). Half the profits went to the owners, the other half to the officers and crew. A large crew was necessary to put aboard captured enemy ships to sail them to port.

The *Chasseur's* original owner hired Kemp to build a trading vessel, not a privateer. After several unsuccessful years in trading, its owner put the ship up for auction. Kemp was one of seventeen men who came together to purchase the *Chasseur* with plans to transform it from a fast trade vessel into an even faster privateer.

A rare engraving of an early shipyard in Philadelphia, similar to those in Fells Point. The twenty-eight-gun frigate *Philadelphia* is under construction.

They added cannons, hired a crew of 148 men, and appointed a captain named William Wade. The *Chasseur* sailed to the Caribbean, then to Europe. The crew captured eleven vessels, sending six to the United States as prizes and burning the other five at sea. Although owning shares in a privateer was risky due to the unpredictable nature of privateering, it could be lucrative.

Thomas Kemp had grown up surrounded by ships. His ancestors, from Yorkshire in England, had settled on the eastern shore of the Chesapeake Bay in 1678. This was an area of never-ending sea grasses and mudflats, where the constant rising and falling of the tides had carved a jagged edge of inlets and coves. Their home sat near the town of St. Michaels, Maryland, which was fast developing into a shipbuilding center. Young Thomas would have heard pounding hammers and creaking beams as shipwrights carved and molded giant pieces of timber into large ships.

In August 1814, the *Chasseur's* captain, Thomas Boyle, boldly sailed into the English Channel. To the shock of the British public, he had written a pronouncement and sent a captured British sailor to attach it to the door of Lloyd's Coffee House in London, then the center of the British insurance industry, a famous haunt of sailors. It proclaimed that all of Britain was thenceforth under a total blockade, an action he could in no way enforce. But to the wonder of all, Boyle captured fourteen British merchant ships during this three-month voyage, returning to Baltimore even more famous than when he left.

Privateer Captain Thomas Boyle created this proclamation in 1814 to strike fear throughout Great Britain.

Perhaps the sights and sounds got into his blood and spurred him on his career path. When he grew older, Thomas served as an apprentice at one of these shipyards.

In 1803, he decided to seek his fortune away from the Eastern Shore. He moved to Baltimore to practice his newly acquired trade and found work in the shipyard of Joseph Sterett that first year. The Sterett shipyard had built the U.S. Frigate *Constellation*, the second warship in the American navy.

Thomas married Sophia Horstman and purchased a house on the corner of Market and Lancaster streets from his father-in-law.

During his first two years in Baltimore, he mostly repaired vessels. But Thomas was eager to start designing and building his own ships. In 1804, he and his brother, Joseph, built the *Thomas and Joseph* schooner, considered the very first schooner he designed.

By 1805, at age twenty-six, Kemp had saved enough money to establish his own shipyard. He purchased land at Washington and Alisanna Streets, and in 1807 he began designing and building ships, almost exclusively Baltimore schooners. Even the U.S. Navy sought his expertise. His yard built two ships for the navy, the USS *Erie* and the USS *Ontario*. Kemp also crafted the masts and spars for the nearly completed frigate *Java*. Business was soon thriving. Kemp's weekly payroll was $1,000 (at a time when skilled workmen earned about $3 per day!).

Kemp's household was growing along with his business. One way historians can learn how many people lived in a household is to look at census records. The U.S. national census data is gathered every ten years. An 1810 census entry lists Thomas Kemp and his wife and three children under the age of ten. It also includes a male between sixteen and twenty-six years old. Except for the head of the household, the census does not list any names, only numbers of people in various age categories. Like Mary Pickersgill, Kemp employed an indentured servant. Most likely the male was Thomas Jones. His indenture papers survived and state that in October 1805 Thomas, of Dorchester County, "doth voluntarily, and of his own free Will and Accord, put himself apprentice to Thos Kemp of the city of Baltimore to learn his Art, Trade and Mystery, and after the Manner of an Apprentice to serve him . . ." As Thomas Kemp had done in his youth, Thomas Jones (or his parents) sought a tradesman to teach him a skill. In return for his service to Kemp, "the said

Master [Kemp] shall use the utmost of his Endeavour to teach or cause to be taught or instructed the said Apprentice in the Trade or Mystery of a shipwright . . ." Kemp agreed to provide the apprentice with sufficient meat, drink, apparel, lodging, and washing fitting for an Apprentice—plus two months of day schooling per year. In return, Jones agreed to serve Kemp, keep his secrets, and obey his "lawful Commands."

The 1810 census record also indicates seven enslaved persons in the Kemp household. Many of Baltimore's largest shipyards utilized slave labor. In 1800, the average shipbuilder in Baltimore owned between five and six slaves. Kemp was raised in the Quaker faith, and Quakers believed in nonviolence and equality. Although many Quakers did not believe slavery was morally acceptable, some did own slaves. There is no additional information about the people Kemp owned.

Kemp's business was booming and was so good that in May 1814, he purchased a 170-acre (68.8 ha) estate in Baltimore called Lovely Green. If the British captured Baltimore, they would most assuredly set fire to the shipyards and possibly confiscate his home. Everything Kemp had worked so hard for could go up in flames. Yet Kemp's success was a major reason why the British hated Baltimore!

CHAPTER

4

THE GREAT BANDIT

In early August 1814, British Rear Admiral George Cockburn (pronounced "COE-burn" in Britain) was expecting his new commanding officer and reinforcements. For more than a year he had been the top military officer in the Chesapeake Bay region and he had wreaked havoc on the area, making sure the Americans knew who was in control.

Rear Admiral George Cockburn in London, 1819. He became famous in England as the man who burned the American capital.

Cockburn, forty-two, hailed from an old Scottish family. He was thrilled to be getting reinforcements. The new forces would swell the British armada to more than fifty ships and strike even more fear into the hearts of the weak Americans.

Not that they weren't already afraid. Cockburn had been busy the previous year, building a reputation and ensuring that people knew his name. His actions had earned him the title of "most hated and feared man in the United States." Only ten days after entering the Chesapeake, he had boasted to his superior that "I have no hesitation in pronouncing that the whole of the shores and towns within this vast bay, not excepting the Capital itself will be wholly at your mercy . . . or destroyed at your pleasure."

The HMS *Canopus*, captured from the French in battle, shows the approximate size of Cockburn's ship.

American newspapers called him "The Great Bandit" and the Boston *Gazette* wrote: "There breathes not in any quarter of the globe a more savage monster than [Cockburn] . . . He is a disgrace to England and to human nature." The *Niles' Weekly Register* cried, "This Cockburn is one of the vilest creatures in existence." He had ravaged and torched the Virginia and Maryland countryside in a war of terror. When his troops approached a private farm, the owners had a choice: They could sell supplies to the British at a low rate and risk being labeled by their neighbors as helping the enemy. Or, they could resist, and the British would confiscate their livestock and food items and maybe torch the property. In Cockburn's thinking, if a town or individual resisted and refused to surrender, he considered it a fortified enemy post and therefore he was free to destroy it and take whatever property he wanted.

His floating castle, the HMS *Albion,* a seventy-four-gun frigate, was larger and more powerful than any other warship sailing the water. Its crew numbered 620 and its support fleet included nearly two dozen sloops, brigs, and tenders.

Cockburn liked being feared. His commanders had ordered him to take the offensive and use his sea power to damage the morale of the Americans. They had chosen a man who had been groomed from a young age for a life in the Royal Navy. His parents had sent him to sea at age fourteen on a navy sloop. By age twenty he had been promoted to an officer and would soon command his first ship, *Speedy.* His superiors had sent him with his fleet to the Chesapeake because they hoped it would force the Americans to divert troops from the Canadian battles. His tasks included blockading the ports and harbors of the 200-mile- (321.87 km) long bay, disrupting American shipping and trade, halting privateering traffic, and gathering intelligence on the area to aid in future attacks.

The Chesapeake was one of America's main waterways, and since roads were generally in horrible condition, water was the fastest way to travel. The young British soldiers new to America were not impressed with the wide, relatively shallow bay. On the *Diadem,* eighteen-year-old Lieutenant George

GREAT BRITAIN.
Union Jack.
20

The national flag of the United Kingdom, called the Union Jack, was adopted in 1801. It combines the flags of England, Scotland, and the red cross of Saint Patrick for Ireland.

Robert Gleig of the Eighty-Fifth Regiment kept a journal. He wrote, "The coast of America, at least in this quarter, is universally low and uninteresting . . . forests of pines appear to rise . . . out of the water. It is also dangerous, from the numerous shoals and sand-banks which run out, in many places, to a considerable extent into the sea . . . This noble bay is far too wide, and the land on each side, too flat to permit any but an indistinct glimpse of the shore, from the deck of a vessel which keeps well towards the middle."

As Cockburn's forces sailed throughout the bay, they took depth measurements to ensure the water was deep enough for large ships to navigate, assessed enemy fortifications, tracked American troops, and noted suitable harbors for large ships. The bay region also held some very juicy targets: Washington, D.C.,

Conditions on the ships of the line, the largest ships in the British navy, were cramped even for junior officers. Lieutenant George Gleig on the *Diadem* was crowded into a cabin with forty other junior officers. But they had it good compared with the enlisted men and seamen jammed together in quarters belowdecks. Historian Walter Lord described their living situation: "Hot, damp, dark, smelly—their life was all that and worse. For food, there was usually just salt beef, tough as mahogany; cheese so hard it could be made into buttons; and biscuits so full of insect life that before eating, the men would tap them on the table to shake out the bugs."

The British sailors needed to check the depth on a regular basis to determine if the water was deep enough to allow access for their large ships.

and its navy yard; a large naval station at Gosport, Virginia; Maryland's capital city, Annapolis; and of course, Baltimore, with its large shipyards and flourishing flour and tobacco trade.

Through ongoing hit-and-run raids beginning in March, Cockburn's sailors destroyed property in towns along the coast. "Go on, my boys, knock down, burn, and destroy," he told his men. His troops, though, did not necessarily agree with his tactics. While he usually stayed within the rules of war, his intent was to show no mercy. He wanted to break the will of the people to fight. He instructed the troops to burn a house if they determined the owner was in the militia. Since most people owned guns for hunting, most houses contained one. To Cockburn, a gun meant a militia member. Torch the house! As one midshipman wrote "every man's house was food for a bonfire."

Map of

CHESAPEAKE
BAY

MAP KEY
- - - - - Key's journey
★ Key and Skinner meet British

0   20

MILES

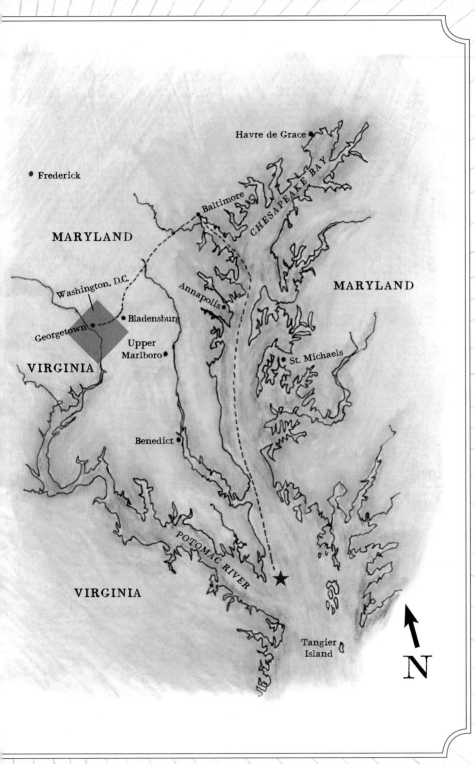

Havre de Grace

Frederick

MARYLAND

CHESAPEAKE BAY

Washington, D.C.

Baltimore

Annapolis

MARYLAND

Georgetown

Bladensburg

Upper
Marlboro

St. Michaels

VIRGINIA

Benedict

POTOMAC RIVER

VIRGINIA

Tangier
Island

N

ADMIRAL COCKBURN BURNING & PLUN
on the 1ˢᵗ of June 1813. done from a Sketch taken

1. *Cockburn.*
2. *Westfall 1ˢᵗ Lieuᵗ of the Marlborough.*
3. *Weyburn Capᵗ of Marines.*
4. *Lieuᵗ Carter.*

G HAVRE DE GRACE
Spot at the time.

     5. *Machine for throwing Rockets.*
     6. *A New Couch part of the Plunder.*
     7. *Mrs Seers Tavern.*
     8. *A British Officer endeavouring to ride over 2 of the Citizens.*

Admiral Cockburn's troops attacked Havre de Grace, Maryland, on June 1, 1813.
Cockburn is the officer front, center. This engraving was based on a sketch
drawn on the spot.

Another soldier wrote, "It is hateful to see the poor Yankees [Americans] robbed, and to be the robber. If we should take fairly it would not be so bad, but the rich escape; for the loss of a few cows and oxen is nothing to a rich man, while you ruin a poor peasant if you take his only cow." He added, "There are numbers of officers, of the navy in particular, whose families are American, and their fathers in one or two instances are . . . living in the very towns we are trying to burn."

Admiral Cockburn's name was well-known. He brimmed with confidence which came across as haughtiness to some. One army lieutenant wrote "Cockburn's confidence in his luck is the very thing to be most feared. It is worse than 1000 Yankees." Cocky to some, he was witty and swashbuckling to others. Fifteen-year-old Midshipman Robert Barrett aboard the HMS *Hebrus* had mixed feelings. He was still new to the navy, having joined in December 1813. Barrett came from a naval family. His father, a captain, had drowned three years earlier in a shipwreck. The British admiral made a huge impression on him. He recalled years later: "It is almost impossible to depict my boyish feelings and [joy] when . . . I gazed, for the first time in my life, on the features of that undaunted seaman, Rear-Admiral George Cockburn, with his sunburnt [face], and his rusty gold-laced hat—an officer who never spared himself, either night or day, but shared on every occasion, the same toil, danger, and privation of the [men] under his command. These are the men who win a gallant sailor's heart!"

☆ ☆ ☆

On August 14, Cockburn spotted the flag of his new commander Vice Admiral Alexander Cochrane's ship, the HMS *Tonnant*. The combined British fleet now became a mightier armada. To Gleig, the sight was "as grand and imposing as any I ever beheld; because one could not help remembering that this powerful fleet was sailing in the enemy's bay, and was filled with troops for the invasion of that enemy's country." Gleig's journal identified the force as consisting of a "battalion of seven hundred marines, an hundred negroes lately armed and [trained], and a division of marine artillery . . ."

☆ ☆ ☆

Portrait of a British midshipman, John Windham Dalling of the Royal Navy, painted after 1805. Midshipmen were typically between the ages of fifteen and twenty-two.

A rumor swept through Cochrane's fleet that Cockburn had recruited fugitive slaves to help fight the Americans. It was no rumor, though. It was true. The Chesapeake region featured good farming land and many farmers had become wealthy by growing tobacco, a crop in great demand in Europe. The crop's cultivation was labor intensive and required constant care. A cruel economic system relying on slave labor had taken root and flourished, based on the import of captive people from Africa. In Great Britain, Parliament had outlawed the international slave trade, but slavery was still legal. The American government, too, had outlawed the importation of slaves and all of the northern states had either abolished slavery or set measures in place to abolish it. But in both Maryland and Virginia, the ownership of humans was legal and, sadly, it had become a foundation of the economy, deeply rooted and widespread.

When Cockburn's ships had first entered the bay the previous year, the British were under orders not to stir emotions or encourage slave revolts. If slaves came to them seeking freedom, military orders dictated that officers aid them and offer protection and the opportunity to resettle in a place they would be free. According to Maryland and Virginia law at the time, slaves were considered property, so helping slaves to escape was equal to stealing.

Only a few decades earlier, during the American Revolution, the British had promised freedom to runaway slaves in the region. With the British arrival in the Chesapeake, the Union Jack flag again symbolized the hope of freedom. Word spread quickly among the enslaved communities. Slaves desiring freedom faced several options. They could escape and flee to the British and request protection. If caught during the attempt, they faced certain punishment. Fleeing to the British required trust that they would in fact be offered a new way of life and not taken someplace like the Caribbean and sold back into slavery. It also meant they may never see their families again. It was usually more complicated and dangerous for groups of slaves to escape at the same time. If they chose not to escape, they had no idea if they would find a future opportunity to gain freedom.

Aiding slaves was viewed by many British officers primarily as a war tactic and not a humanitarian endeavor. For the British, there was a cost to welcoming the runaways. Often slaves arrived at British ships with no personal items and little clothing. The British needed to feed and clothe them and to ensure their freedom, which meant transporting them away from the area. Every day the British were in the Chesapeake, enslaved people found their way to British ships. As a military tactic, the British decided to use the existence of slavery to their advantage. Freeing the slaves would hurt the local economy. But another idea took hold, one that would inflict more damage on the Americans.

The navy's leadership decided to use these fugitive slaves to bolster their numbers of fighting forces. Based in the Caribbean a few years earlier, Vice Admiral Cochrane had successfully recruited a force of former slaves. He quickly realized that besides providing more fighting troops, training former slaves to fight could serve as a significant psychological blow to southern slave owners. Laws prohibited slaves from carrying guns or serving in the military. The fact that the British were using their "property" against them would unsettle the Americans. The former slaves also knew the land and could provide valuable information to aid British movement.

That spring, Cochrane had ordered Cockburn to "find and get possession of some convenient island or point within the Chesapeake . . . which might serve as a place of refuge for the negro slaves from the surrounding shores." Cockburn selected Tangier Island, a small, sandy island sitting in the middle of the bay east of the mouth of the Potomac River. Its location provided easy access for both the upper and lower parts of the bay and to the enslaved communities in the region. The island became a base for refugees and later a training camp and barracks for the black soldiers.

By the end of May 1814, the troops had built Fort Albion on that tiny spit of sand in the middle of the sparkling Chesapeake. Named for Cockburn's flagship, and the ancient name for England, its cluster of buildings eventually included barracks, a church, a hospital, and dwellings with gardens. It became a temporary home to almost one thousand escaped slaves who fled to freedom.

A modern illustration of a British Colonial Marine depicted in uniform around 1814.

The new recruits would form the Corps of the Colonial Marines. Cockburn didn't think many escaped slaves would choose to join the military and was doubtful as to their usefulness in this capacity. At first, he claimed that the refugees were "naturally neither very valorous [courageous] nor very active." But as he watched the first eighty recruits train, he gradually changed his mind. He soon boasted that the new troops "are getting on astonishingly and are really very fine fellows." He admitted "they have induced me to alter the bad opinion I had of the whole of their Race and I now really believe these, we are training, will neither show want of zeal or courage when employed by us in attacking their old Masters."

The Colonial Marines had their first test in battle at the end of May 1814 and their commander later reported that the "new . . . Black Corps . . . gave a most excellent specimen of what they are likely to be, their conduct was marked by great spirit and vivacity."

BY The Honorable Sir *ALEXANDER COCHRANE*,
K. B. *Vice Admiral of the Red, and Commander in
Chief of His Majesty's Ships and Vessels, upon the
North American Station, &c. &c. &c.*

A PROCLAMATION.

WHEREAS it has been represented to me, that many Persons now resident in the UNITED STATES, have expressed a desire to withdraw therefrom, with a view of entering into His Majesty's Service, or of being received as Free Settlers into some of His Majesty's Colonies.

This is therefore to Give Notice,

That all those who may be disposed to emigrate from the UNITED STATES will, with their Families, be received on board of His Majesty's Ships or Vessels of War, or at the Military Posts that may be established, upon or near the Coast of the UNITED STATES, when they will have their choice of either entering into His Majesty's Sea or Land Forces, or of being sent as FREE Settlers, to the British Possessions in North America or the West Indies, where they will meet with all due encouragement.

*GIVEN under my Hand at Bermuda, this
2nd day of April,* 1814.
ALEXANDER COCHRANE.

By Command of the Vice Admiral,
WILLIAM BALHETCHET.
1609
GOD SAVE THE KING.

Cochrane issued this proclamation on April 2, 1814, directly to the enslaved population promising freedom and the choice of military service or resettlement.

As the British had predicted, the prospect of freed slaves fighting for the British against their former masters horrified many Americans. One newspaper was outraged at the savagery of the "Great Bandit Cockburn" and his "negroes in uniform." For his part, Cockburn wrote to his superior that "the Colonial Marines, who were for the first time, employed in Arms against their old Masters . . . behaved to the admiration of every Body." By midsummer, 120 men had enlisted, and the force would eventually reach almost 250.

Not all escaped slaves sided with the British.
Charles Ball enlisted with the Americans. Years later, he published a book describing his experiences during the war. Born into slavery on a tobacco farm in Maryland, Ball was about twelve when his owner died. Enslaved people had no control over their lives, and often owners sold slaves due to financial difficulties. To settle debts, Ball's family was sold, and he was brutally separated from his mother. Years later, his owner sold him to someone in Georgia. Charles managed to escape and follow the stars north back to his wife and children in Calvert County, Maryland. Proclaiming himself a free man, he found work as a farmer and a fisherman. Charles witnessed the terror inflicted by Cockburn's troops when the British attacked a fishery where he worked. Describing a different attack, he wrote: "The lieutenant . . . went up to the house of a farmer . . . and after pilfering the premises of every thing that he could carry away, set fire to the house, and returned to his boat. In the course of the summer and fall of the year 1813, I witnessed many other atrocities, of equal enormity." In December 1813, Ball enlisted with the Chesapeake Flotilla as seaman and cook. He fought with this group at Bladensburg and noted the impressive appearance of the British officers, writing "I thought then, and think yet, that General Ross was one of the finest looking men that I ever saw on horseback." He mentioned his involvement in the Battle of Baltimore but did not provide any details. After the war, slave catchers tracked Ball down and dragged him back to Georgia, but he escaped again. His autobiography titled *Slavery in the United States: A Narrative of the Life and Adventures of Charles Ball, a Black Man*, first published in 1837, offers a shocking account of Ball's amazing life.

A modern illustration of Charles Ball dressed in an American uniform. He served in the Chesapeake Flotilla and at Bladensburg and Baltimore.

A modern illustration of Colonial Marines training on Tangier Island.

One person who joined the Colonial Marines was Ezekiel Loney, a twenty-seven year old working the Corotoman plantation in northern Virginia. When British barges ventured near the plantation, the person in charge of the slaves ordered them to scatter into the woods in fear that they would escape to the enemy. Three young men, including Ezekiel Loney, seized the opportunity and did just that. Often, young men who managed to escape wanted to rescue family and friends as well. Four days after Loney escaped, he returned in the early hours of the morning with British soldiers to free a total of sixty-nine enslaved individuals, the largest number that escaped from a Chesapeake Bay area plantation at one time during the war.

The Americans kept watch on waterways and tried to prevent slaves from going to the British. Some slave owners even visited British ships under a flag of truce to try to convince their former slaves to return to them. The British encouraged the masters to do so, to counter any charges that the British captured slaves by force, but insisted that the ex-slaves should decide their own fate. A British officer was required to be present at all times. The captain assembled the fugitives on deck and announced "Your masters come for you, you are at liberty to follow them, but recollect that you are as free as themselves." Rarely were the slave owners successful. Until they established the base at Tangier Island, the British generally sent the refugees first to their base in Bermuda, and later to the colony of Nova Scotia. They employed them on navy projects and paid them a minimal wage.

The whole enterprise was ironic given the fact that the English had brought slavery to the New World and it was still legal in most of the British Empire. For this brief moment, however, while the British sailed the Chesapeake, they represented the hope of freedom to the enslaved communities who dared escape and come to them. While the British could boldly claim they would free slaves, the reality of limited food and clothing, along with people who didn't want them in Bermuda and Nova Scotia meant life in this new freedom would not be easy.

Despite the successful creation of the base on Tangier Island, Cockburn's immediate concern was preparation for military victory and he was convinced that a target in the near future should be Baltimore. The black troops could help his effort.

CHAPTER

5

UNDER A FLAG OF TRUCE

I n early August, Francis Scott Key, called Frank by his family and friends, was worried about the safety of his family—his six children (all under eleven years old) and his wife, Polly. They lived in Georgetown, a port on the Potomac River, not far from Washington. If the British decided to attack the nation's capital city, that was too close for comfort. Polly, however, refused to leave. After much discussion between them, they ended up sending the children north to stay with their grandparents near Frederick, Maryland, about fifty miles northwest of

Frank Key came from a long line of lawyers. His great-grandfather Philip Key practiced law in London, then left England in 1720 to seek his fortune in the colonies. He ended up in Maryland, building a thriving law practice there. Five of his six sons became lawyers, including Francis Key, Frank Key's grandfather and namesake. Undated wood engraving of Key.

Washington. And in a compromise, Polly agreed to stay with friends who lived halfway between Georgetown and Frederick.

Frank, a thirty-five-year-old lawyer, had been adamantly opposed to "this abominable war" when it began. He wasn't against war in general, just this one. His father, John, had fought for Maryland in the Continental Army (alongside Sam Smith).

Frank had grown up listening to war stories, including one about the 1781 siege of Yorktown and the resulting British surrender. His father even claimed to have fought under the command of the famous French major general the Marquis de Lafayette. His father's brother, Uncle Philip, however, had joined the British army and fought for General Sir Henry Clinton. The General Court of Maryland ultimately found him and other Marylanders who had fought with loyalist regiments guilty of treason. He was sent to prison in the Caribbean and later, upon being released, managed to go to England. He ended up studying law in London and returning to America four years later where, surprisingly, he was welcomed back by his family.

Uncle Philip had settled in Georgetown and started a law practice. Years later, his neighbors elected him to the House of Representatives and he had turned his law practice over to Frank, who ran it out of his home on Bridge Street.

Key had been horrified in 1812 when the American military went on the offensive and invaded Canada. But in 1813, increasing British military activity around the Chesapeake Bay had caused Frank to rethink his opposition to the war. He read in the newspapers and heard the talk about the Great Bandit Cockburn. The offensive war had suddenly turned defensive. Frank believed in defending one's country and wanted to do something to help his community. In July of that year he enlisted briefly with a field artillery militia formed by a Georgetown friend. Nine months later he rejoined the group as a quartermaster, an officer's rank.

In August 1814, Frank found himself at Bladensburg. His limited military experience and lack of military training hardly prepared him to be in the Maryland town, near Washington,

Like Mary Pickersgill, Thomas Kemp, and Samuel Smith, Frank Key owned slaves—ironic for the man who wrote that the United States was the "land of the free." Key grew up in a slave-owning family and purchased his first slave at age twenty-one or twenty-two. His wife, Mary "Polly" Tayloe (Lloyd) Key, was a member of one of Maryland's largest and most powerful landholding families. Her father owned hundreds of slaves and thousands of acres, including Wye Plantation on the Eastern Shore where future abolitionist and orator Frederick Douglass was born, enslaved.

Key was a man of contradictions when it came to people of African heritage. He earned a reputation for providing legal advice to free blacks at no charge and was an early and tireless opponent of the slave trade. He freed at least seven of his slaves during his lifetime. But as a U.S. attorney for Washington, D.C., he opposed abolitionists (people who wanted to get rid of slavery) and enforced laws against African Americans.

Key was also a leading proponent of colonization, a controversial movement that encouraged former slaves and other African American men and women to leave the United States and settle, free, in Africa. In the 1800s some people thought this was a solution to ease tension between the races. They could not envision an America where African Americans could become citizens. Key spoke at the founding meeting of the American Society for Colonizing the Free People of Color on December 21, 1816 (later called the American Colonization Society). Samuel Smith was also an advocate for colonization and active in the Maryland State Colonization Society.

when the British attacked. With the British headed toward Washington, Frank had volunteered as an aide to General Walter Smith, the commander of the First Columbian Brigade, a reserve force of men from Georgetown. Perhaps Smith asked for Frank's help since he knew the terrain around Bladensburg. In any case, Frank ended up contributing very little to the lackadaisical American effort and was embarrassed by their lack of discipline. Frank went home to Georgetown and nursed his pride.

His relationship with the British was about to get much more personal.

On August 27, some British soldiers returning to their ships after Bladensburg had raided farms in Maryland, including one owned by Dr. William Beanes, a friend of Frank's and a leading physician in Upper Marlboro. Beanes organized a group of men to go after the renegade soldiers. They captured several of the soldiers and threw them in a local jail. One escaped, gathered several other British soldiers, and planned to retaliate. They burst into Beanes' home at midnight, forced him and two others out of bed, put them on horses, and made them ride thirty-five miles to the British troops at Benedict.

For whatever reason, the British soon released the other two, but kept sixty-five-year-old Beanes. They put him aboard the brig HMS *Thetis*. His friends knew they had to act fast to save him. They rushed a letter signed by the Maryland governor to General Robert Ross at British headquarters. He ignored it. Beanes' friends then decided to try a different approach. They would need someone persuasive who could make a strong case to the top British generals for Beanes' release. They knew just the person.

As a lawyer, Frank Key knew how to be persuasive. When

Frank argued his first case in front of the Supreme Court of the United States, newspapers had said he "addressed the court in the most impressive and eloquent manner." Soon after, he was in the national newspapers again when he defended a U.S. senator from Ohio in front of the entire Senate. He'd also represented the Jefferson administration in another case before the Supreme Court. Key had been gradually building a reputation as a "first-rate legal mind." As one observer wrote to the *Baltimore Federal Republican,* "His quickness, his address, his power of retort and insinuation, combined with an irresistible force of solid argumentation render him almost unrivaled, and certainly rank him among the most pleasing, chaste, able and classical speakers of the age in which we live."

Beanes' friends, including Frank's brother-in-law Richard West, rode to Georgetown to plead with Frank to intervene. He agreed to lend his legal skills to the cause. This was no easy undertaking. In order to meet with the British, he had to secure permission from President Madison and from General John Mason, commissioner general in charge of matters relating to military prisoners. They both complied, in part because Beanes was not a soldier and, under terms of war, should not have been taken prisoner. Mason gave Key a letter to deliver to the British leaders demanding Beanes' release and calling his emissary, Key, "a citizen of the highest respectability." The letter stated that Beanes had been "taken from his bed, in the midst of his family and hurried off almost without clothes." This seizure was "a departure from the known usages of civilized warfare."

Mason had also contacted the senior British prisoner and informed him that a truce ship would be traveling to the British leadership. He offered to deliver "any open letters that you

John Stuart Skinner accompanied Frank Key to negotiate with the British. Based in Baltimore, after the war he served as the city's postmaster. This portrait was made in 1825.

or any of the prisoners may choose to send to the British army." This humanitarian gesture of allowing prisoners to communicate with their comrades may have had a political motive. It could help sway the decision to release Beanes in the Americans' favor.

On September 2, Frank wrote to his mother "I am going in the morning to Baltimore to proceed in a flag vessel to General Ross. Old Dr. Beanes of Marbro [Marlboro] is taken prisoner by the Enemy, who threaten to carry him off. Some of his friends have urged me to apply for a flag [of truce] and go & try to procure his release. I hope to return in about 8 or 10 days, though it is uncertain as I do not know where to find the fleet." He promised to join the family in Frederick as soon as he returned.

Frank traveled the 40 miles (64.37 km) to Baltimore where he met up with John Skinner who would accompany him on his mission. Skinner worked for General Mason and was responsible for prisoner exchanges. At age twenty-six, he had a surprising amount of experience dealing with the British and was a veteran of many missions to communicate between the two countries. He was not optimistic of success. Skinner was as familiar as anyone in America with Cockburn and knew him to be uncompromising. They set off on September 5 in a 60-foot (18.29 m) sloop, named USS *President*, looking for the British fleet. Under a safe-conduct flag, the boat sailed past Fort McHenry and down the bay.

While this type of negotiation with the enemy over prisoners was rather common during wartime, Frank had never done this before. Beanes, as a civilian, should not have been captured, was there a chance that Frank could be too?

CHAPTER

6

A PLAN OF ACTION

The day the British burned Washington, August 25, Baltimore's city council called an emergency meeting. The big question at hand was: If the British show up, should the city surrender without a fight or should it defend itself? Of course, they couldn't know the British intentions—occupy the city or burn it. Many influential citizens thought it would be crazy to fight the powerful British. They claimed that surrender would preserve the city and save lives. In the end, those calling for defense won the argument.

Another group, the Committee of Vigilance and Safety, made up of thirty or so community members, also convened to discuss the city's defense preparations. Thousands of militia men from across Maryland and the neighboring states of Pennsylvania and Virginia had been pouring into Baltimore. Who would lead these volunteer soldiers from other states and those in the regular army? Brigadier General William Winder had led the American forces' disastrous effort the day before in D.C. and everyone had lost confidence in him. Even being the governor's nephew didn't help him now.

A delegation of military officers came forward to recommend Samuel Smith for the job of officer in charge of all militias and federal troops. Major General Samuel Smith, also a U.S. senator, was the highest-ranking military man in the state militia. Smith, a leading citizen of Baltimore, had already been directing the city's efforts to beef up its security. The vigilance committee officially offered Smith the command of the city's defense.

Samuel Smith painted by famed artist Rembrandt Peale three years after the Battle of Baltimore.

He responded: "My friends I have but one life to lose, and that, I have at all times been willing to hazard in defense of my beloved country. Tell the members of your convention that I willingly obey their call, and, confidently expect their hearty cooperation in every necessary means of defense."

Smith was the ideal choice for many reasons. To begin with, he had a long history of interaction with the British. He was born in 1752 in Carlisle, Pennsylvania, then the frontier. His grandfather had emigrated to Lancaster County, Pennsylvania, from County Tyrone in Northern Ireland. At that time, the British were fighting the French and Indian War; young Smith observed various military activities. At one point, the Smith home even served as headquarters for a British general. When Smith was seven, his father moved the family to Baltimore, then a town of fewer than one thousand families. His father built a wharf and warehouse and started a shipping business. It flourished, and at age fourteen, Sam joined the business as a clerk. At nineteen, he traveled to Europe and lived in London where for a time he represented the business. In 1774, he received a letter from his father making him a partner and calling him back to Baltimore.

His relationship with the British changed suddenly when a

Samuel Smith fought in the American Revolution from 1776 to 1779 and rose in rank from captain to lieutenant colonel. He fought in many major engagements of the war, including the battles of Long Island, Monmouth, and Brandywine. He served with John Ross Key, a year younger than him, and the future father of Francis Scott Key. One of Smith's major assignments would give him valuable experience for his future efforts in Baltimore. In October 1777, General Washington designated Smith the senior commander in charge of Fort Mifflin, which sat on the Delaware River and guarded the water access to Philadelphia from the south. The British occupied the city, but were surrounded by patriot forces on all sides except the south. They desperately needed supplies from their ships sitting in the Delaware Bay, but Fort Mifflin was standing in the way. They would attack the fort. Smith's superiors ordered him and his force to hold off the British as long as possible to allow Washington's army to get settled in winter quarters at Valley Forge, west of the city. Smith's troops forced a six-week battle, the largest bombardment in the revolution. The British ships fired 238 cannons to the fort's ten. Four hundred Americans held off a British force of two thousand. Ultimately, Smith and his men safely abandoned the fort, but their perseverance had earned them great respect and had bought the Continental Army the time it desperately needed.

year later they became the enemy. The war for independence from Britain began and Smith joined the local militia, the Baltimore Independent Cadets, the first uniformed company in Maryland. He quickly rose in rank and his unit traveled north to aid General Washington in the fight against the British. Smith spent four years fighting in the American Revolution.

In 1779, Smith resigned his military commission to help his family business deal with the financial challenges brought on by the war. Smith and Sons briefly went into the privateering business. Their privateers captured about a dozen enemy vessels, which allowed them to expand their fleet.

Smith also decided it was time to get married and start a family. He and Margaret Spear wed and soon their household was noisy with an increasing number of children. They eventually had twelve! He spent a lot of time working to expand the family shipping business and by the end of the 1780s he owned twenty ships, a distillery, a store in Baltimore, warehouses, wharves, several houses, and slaves. The Smiths also built a country estate they named Montebello, overlooking Baltimore.

During this time of peace, Smith decided to try his hand at national politics. The people of Baltimore elected him to represent them first in the House of Representatives and then in the Senate, where he eventually became president pro tempore, the second-highest-ranking member of the Senate. Smith was well-respected and was connected to all the leading officials of Baltimore.

In 1814, Smith was the perfect person to lead Baltimore's defense. At sixty-two, he had a lot of life experience. Besides a history with the British, Revolutionary War experience, political and business connections, and his long family history in Baltimore, Smith had already offered a strategic vision for the city's defense. In June 1812, Senator Smith had voted for America to declare war on Britain. He then returned to Baltimore from Washington to organize the city's defenses . . . just in case the enemy came close. Under his direction, the city strengthened Fort McHenry, adding larger cannons with longer range to keep attacking ships farther out at sea. Smith successfully lobbied for a new commander for the fort, thirty-three-year-old Major George Armistead, and set up a plan for training the militias. Smith also oversaw the preparation of defense structures on Hampstead Hill, the high point east of the city, positioning fifty cannons on the hill and building earth walls. He also initiated a regional intelligence network and directed the reconnoitering of the North Point area, a probable landing spot for British troops.

These preparations proved wise. Although the war raged in the far north, the British navy in the bay kept reminding Baltimore citizens of its presence. Cockburn's squadron had sailed near Baltimore doing research for a possible attack: taking depth findings and noting Fort McHenry's layout. In a show of power, for three weeks the British blockaded the city's harbor. Then they left, only to make return appearances later in 1813. Nervous American militia stood by for weeks.

Thus, Smith's selection again as overall commander of Baltimore's defenses signaled the city's renewed confidence that Smith would do what was necessary to ensure its safety and freedom. Washington had been caught by surprise but Baltimore would be ready.

If the reports were true and the British were headed their way, time was running out. Smith put a plan into action. He predicted

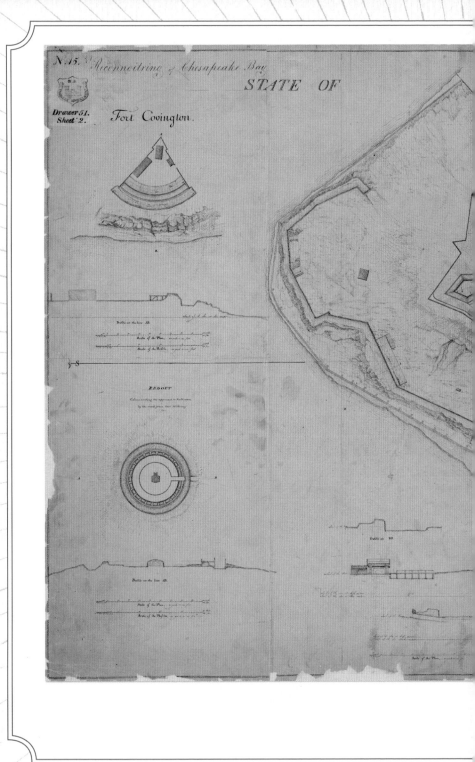

Reconnoitring of Chesapeake Bay

STATE OF

Drawer 51.
Sheet 2.

Fort Covington.

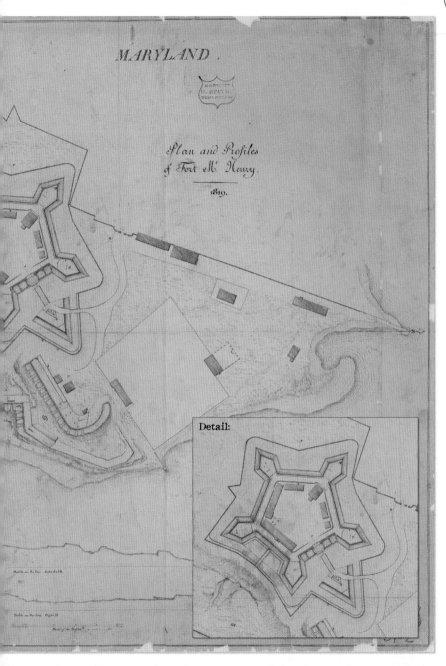

MARYLAND.

*Plan and Profiles
of Fort McHenry.*

1819.

Detail:

Star-shaped forts were thought to be more efficient because their shape offered multiple points for shooting a line of attackers. This plan of Fort McHenry was drawn five years after the battle and clearly shows the star-shaped pattern.

that the British would launch a two-pronged attack: The navy would attack Fort McHenry in an attempt to move into the harbor, and the marines would land at North Point and march toward the city from the east.

To address the water attack and bolster Fort McHenry's power, Smith directed the construction of eleven floating barges, two built by Thomas Kemp's expert carpenters. Each barge held two guns and a crew of thirty-four men, and were stationed around the fort, some within the harbor itself. Smith also directed the construction of a large boom (a chain and masts floating on the water's surface) that was laid across the harbor entrance and near the shores of Fort McHenry to help keep enemy ships from passing. Ultimately, the forces at Fort McHenry (one thousand men and over sixty cannons) would need to withstand whatever barrage the British bomb ships would throw at them.

With advice from his officers, Smith approved an idea to completely block access to the harbor. Careful to notify Baltimore's Committee of Vigilance and Safety, he authorized troops to confiscate a number of privately owned old brigs and schooners and strategically sink them in the narrow harbor entrance. Altogether they sank twenty-four vessels. Andrew Clopper, one of Baltimore's biggest ship owners, borrowed Thomas Kemp's carpenters to contribute to the work. Instead of using their skills at building, they labored at cutting apart ships and a brig to sink them. One by one the ships disappeared beneath the water, the *Columbia, Parkett, Enterprise, Rosanna, Scudder,* the *Father and Son, Eliza, Ann,* and the *Chesapeake.* If the British managed to get past Fort McHenry, their ships would get stuck in a forest of masts.

Smith positioned his main land defense force of over twelve

thousand troops on Hampstead Hill. The high ground offered a tactical advantage that helped outweigh the inexperience of the troops. A French engineer supervised the construction of a 1.5-mile- (2.41 km) long earthwork, a series of trenches and platforms linking forty-eight cannons, part of a larger almost 3-mile (4.83 km) ring of iron totaling one hundred cannons. The Committee of Vigilance and Safety divided the city into four districts and every white man and free black man was required to work with others from their district every fourth day on the fortifications, along with any enslaved men from the district who were forced to do the same. Volunteers from outside the city came from all over to pitch in. All brought wheelbarrows, shovels, and whatever digging equipment they could find. "They are throwing up entrenchments all around the city," reported the *Evening Post*, "White and black are all at work together." The citizens reported at 6:00 a.m. and worked until dark. Even Smith's twelve-year-old nephew, Sam W. Smith, joined the diggers. And again, the military called on Kemp's carpenters to work on the batteries, finishing gun carriages and platforms.

Smith also addressed the little things that came up: The army was running out of bread, so he released the bakers from military service and instructed them to start making biscuits. When traffic choked the streets, he ordered a temporary bridge of scows built across the harbor. When the War Department ordered five cannons at Fort McHenry returned to Washington, Smith investigated and found the cannons were U.S. property but the carriages they rode on were Baltimore city property. He encouraged the city government to make a case against returning the cannons, and the federal government conceded. To finance the surge of activity, Smith convinced the banks to advance $663,000 for the cause. And townspeople donated services and goods, from bricks to shad (fish) and hay.

To the relief of the city leaders, their request for volunteer soldiers from neighboring states had been received and acted upon. Militias from Virginia, Delaware, and Pennsylvania encamped within a 10-mile (16 km) radius of Baltimore. By early September, there were fifteen thousand, with more coming each day, including future U.S. president James Buchanan from Pennsylvania. The quartermasters in Baltimore looked desperately for places to accommodate the troops. They housed them in 1,000-foot- (304.8 m) long ropewalks near Fells Point, warehouses near the docks, and even a Catholic cathedral under construction. Some brought supplies but most did not. Some didn't have shoes; others didn't have knapsacks, cooking kettles, canteens, tents, or even ammunition! And the troops needed food.

Rumors were flying. The British were coming. The British were going. It was hard to keep track of the enemy. One would think it could be a challenge to hide a fifty-boat armada, but the Chesapeake Bay is a huge body of water, with many inlets. Were the British headed to the Atlantic Ocean or staying on the bay? On September 10, Major Armistead, commander of Fort McHenry, wrote to his wife that the British were seen sailing south and leaving the bay, but later that evening word arrived in Baltimore confirming that the British fleet was moving north. What was Smith to do?

American Prizes.

MONTHLY LIST—CONTINUED FROM VOL. VI.

The winds and seas are Britain's wide domain,
And not a sail, but by permission spreads!

British Naval Register.

1098. Brig —, from Madeira for Liverpool, N. S. captured by the Rambler of Boston, on her way to Canton, divested of 80 or 90 casks of wine, and given up.

1099, 1100. A brig and a schooner captured by the late U. S. brig Rattlesnake and sunk.

1101. Brig Fortitude, from Rio Janeiro, with a great cargo of hides, coffee, dye-wood, &c. sent into Union River, Maine, by the Surprize of Baltimore.

1102. Schooner George Canning, from Spain for England, laden with Merino wool and fruit, captured by the Gen. Armstrong of New-York, and sent into Thomastown.

1103. Ship Pizarro, from Liverpool for Amelia Island, with dry goods, crates, copper and salt, sent into Savannah by the Midas of Baltimore.

1104. Brig Espiranza, from Amelia for Havanna, with cotton, rice and flour, sent into ditto by ditto.

1105. Brig Elsinore, from Turks Island for Amelia, with salt, sent into ditto by ditto.

1106, 1107, 1108, 1109. Ship Julia, brig Mary Ann, schooners John Duncan and Louisa, captured by the Harrison of Baltimore, divested of goods to the value of £18,000 sterling, and given up or destroyed.

1110. Schooner —, with a large amount of specie on board, captured by ditto, and manned for the United States.

☞ The Harrison has arrived at Savannah with her rich spoils.

1111. Brig Betsey, with a cargo of fish, from Newfoundland for Barbadoes sent into Boston, by the York of Baltimore.

1112. Ship Alfred, ballast, sent into a southern port by the Harpey of Baltimore.

1113. Ship Antonia under Russian colors, from Lisbon for St. Michaels, laden with dry goods, brandy, and some hard ware and crockery, sent into ditto by ditto.

1114, 1115. Two brigs in ballast, captured by ditto and burnt.

1116. Schooner Henry, with a cargo of fish, from Halifax, captured by the Saratoga, of New-York, (then 4 days out) and sent into New-Bedford.

1117. Packet ———— captured by the Harpey of Baltimore, and divested of 10,000$. The Harpey has arrived at an eastern port. This vessel was the Princess Elizabeth, 8 guns (two long brass 9's &c. 9, 12 lb. gunnades) and 28 men, taken after a warm defence, in which she had some killed and wounded, and was much cut up. She had on board a Turkish ambassador for England; an aid to a British general; and the 2d officer of a 74. She was ransomed for $2,000 after taking from her the specie, and her two brass, and two other guns (the rest being thrown overboard) five pipes of wine, &c. The privateer had one man killed.

1118. Ship Hero from Newfoundland, with 4,855 quintals of cod fish, sent into Hyannis, by the Ida of Boston.

1119. East India company's ship Countess of Harcourt, 520 tons 6 heavy guns and 90 men; outward bound, laden with dry-goods, brandy, rum, gin, &c. &c. separated from the fleet in a gale, and captured in the British channel by the Sabine of Baltimore, and sent into a southern port. This is the first British Indiaman that has visited us for many years. We should like to have a few dozen more of them!

1120. "His majesty's" packet, the cutter Landraile, — guns, 33 men, captured after a hard battle in the British channel, by the Syren of Baltimore, divested, &c. and the prisoners brought to New-York.

1121, 1122, Two brigs captured by the same; one burnt the other released, being divested, &c.

1123, 1124, 1125, 1126, 1127, 1128, 1129, 1130, 1131, 1132, 1133, 1134, 1135, 1136; fourteen enemy vessels, captured in the British channel by the Governor Tompkins of New-York (chiefly owned in Baltimore,) divested of their valuable articles, and burnt. The privateer had also taken six other prizes. We hope to hear further of them.

1137. Brig Betsey and Mary, from Spain for London, with wool, &c. captured by the Kemp of Baltimore, divested of 105 bales merino wool, and burnt.

1138. Ship Calypso, under Swedish colors, with Dutch papers, captured by the same, divested of some part of her cargo and permitted to proceed.

1139. Brig Caledonia, from Bordeaux for Lisbon, also under Swedish colors, but with British papers captured by the same, divested of 30 bales of dry-goods and 3000$ in specie belonging to the paymaster of the 41st regiment (who was paroled) and suffered to proceed.

1140. Brig New-Frederick from Smyrna for Hull, captured by the same, and out of humanity to an Italian lady, permitted to proceed, after divesting her of some articles.

☞ The Kemp has arrived at North Carolina from Nantz, where she completed her cargo, which is exceedingly valuable. She sailed as a letter of marque.

1141. Schooner Contract, laden with salt, sent into North Carolina by the Roger of Norfork.

1142. "His majesty's" transport brig Doris, No. 650, captured by the Grampus of Baltimore, sent into Marblehead. The Doris was from Senegal bound to Portsmouth; and had on board 30 or 40 soldiers; also two elegant horses, one hyena, two jackalls, &c. presents for the prince Regent.

1143, 1144. Ship Hopper, and brig Eliza, from Amelia bound to England with cotton, sent into Savannah by the Saucy Jack of Charleston.

1145, 1146. Two merchantmen captured by the United States brig Syren, and burnt. Particulars not yet known.

1148. "His majesty's" brig Melville, 14 guns, laden with valuable stores, chased ashore on Lake Ontario and destroyed.

As Baltimore prepared for a possible British attack, its privateers were busy around the world harassing British shipping. Every edition of the *Niles' Weekly Register* included a list of prizes captured by American privateers. The *Harrison* of Baltimore, for example, seized five enemy vessels. Can you find others?

CHAPTER

7

NO LOVE FOR AMERICANS

☆ ☆ ☆ ☆ ☆ ☆ ☆ ☆ ☆ ☆ ☆ ☆ ☆ ☆ ☆ ☆ ☆ ☆

As with most summers, a thick soup of hot, humid air engulfed the Chesapeake Bay region the summer of 1814, increasing everyone's irritability. Fifty-six-year-old Vice Admiral Sir Alexander Cochrane—the highest-ranking British officer in North America—hailed from Scotland, a cooler climate. Although he'd been posted around the world, including Egypt and the Caribbean, he found stifling temperatures hard to bear. The heat was suffocating, not to mention the clouds of mosquitos.

Though commander of the British military in North America, Cochrane did not arrive in American waters until August 1814. He had been stationed in Bermuda. This portrait dates to about 1824.

Cochrane wrote a letter to his superiors in England with news of the British sack of Washington. They would be so pleased. While his top general, Robert Ross, and his top admiral, George Cockburn, were urging him to attack Baltimore next, he decided the cooler breezes of the Atlantic would be healthier for his men. "The worst enemy that we have to contend with is the climate—this obliges us to proceed northward," he wrote to his superiors.

He had his sights set on Rhode Island with the intention to return and attack Baltimore in early November when the weather was cooler. "As soon as the army is all reembarked, I mean to proceed to the northward and try to surprise Rhode Island," he wrote to Lord Melville, First Lord of the Admiralty. Then, anticipating fresh troops from England in the near future, he wrote "If the reinforcements arrive I propose an attack upon Baltimore the most democratic town and I believe the richest in the country." The *Iphigenia*, one of the fastest ships in the armada, was at the ready to speed his news across the Atlantic.

The British Admiralty had made Alexander Cochrane commander of the North American station based in Bermuda four months earlier. His initial summer plan for America had been to attack Portsmouth, New Hampshire, or Rhode Island. But he had received a letter from George Cockburn, who had been in the Chesapeake region the previous year. Cochrane had asked for his opinion on where an attack would have the most impact on the Americans. Cockburn had lobbied for Washington, D.C.— why not go for the new country's capital city? The British were still smarting from the Americans' burning of the Canadian capital, York (present-day Toronto), sixteen months prior. Why not give the Americans a taste of their own medicine?

And so, Cochrane had been persuaded to approve Washington. While he had been pleased with the ease of the attack the previous week, Cochrane did not think General Ross had gone far enough. On the water, Ross was under the command of Cochrane, who decided where the expedition would sail and whom it would target. But Ross could "veto" landing his troops and, on land, had full control over them. As the top general, Ross had authority to make final decisions regarding use of the army. Burning the major public buildings had dealt a psychological blow to the Americans, but it had not resulted in much economic damage. Cochrane wanted any future attack on Baltimore to be different and thought the Admiralty in England could put some pressure on Ross to go farther. "As this town [Baltimore] ought to be laid in ashes, some hints ought to be given to Genl. Ross as he does not seem inclined to visit the sins committed upon His Majesty's Canadian subjects upon inhabitants of this state," wrote Cochrane.

Cochrane came from a long line of military officers. He was born in Scotland in 1758, the sixth of eight surviving sons of Sir Thomas Cochrane, eighth Earl of Dundonald. He had followed in the footsteps of earlier generations and joined the navy at age fifteen as a midshipman. He rose fast and earned the rank of lieutenant by age twenty. He had sailed all over the world and spent time in the American colonies during the War for Independence.

Cochrane hated Americans and called them a "corrupt and depraved race." They had killed his brother Charles at the Battle of Yorktown. A major in the army and aide to General Cornwallis, Charles had been standing next to Cornwallis just two days before the British surrendered to the Americans and French. In the midst of battle, his head had been shot off by a cannonball.

When the war officially ended and peace came in 1783, Cochrane had been serving on a ship in New York. During his time in the state, he interacted with many people who had stayed loyal to Britain. His wife, Maria, an American, was from a prominent loyalist family who ended up losing their fortune when their property was confiscated by the rebels, and they were forced to flee to Canada.

By 1794, he captained the frigate *Thetis* operating out of Nova Scotia. There he saw his in-laws living in poverty. The United

States had reneged on its promise to compensate loyalists for their lost property in the Treaty of Paris. This only deepened his hatred of the Americans.

Another reason for his hostility to Americans was a direct encounter he had with the institution of slavery. In the summer of 1794, the *Thetis* had been damaged in a bad storm and he sailed the ship to Norfolk, Virginia, for repairs. There he came into contact with slaves and slaveholders and observed the inhumane nature of slavery and "the burning desire of the slaves to be free."

When he became commander of the North American station, Cochrane began planning an attack on America. On March 10, he wrote that he believed "all the country southwest of the Chesapeake might be restored to the dominion of Great Britain, if under the command of enterprising generals." It was Cochrane's orders, in part, that had spurred Cockburn to bring terror to the Chesapeake. He had written to his senior officers in July: "You are hereby required and directed to destroy and lay waste such towns and districts upon the coast as you may find assailable [vulnerable to attack]."

And Cochrane had come up with the plan to supplement the British military: The Colonial Marines had been his idea.

☆ ☆ ☆

Despite his top commander's insistence to attack Baltimore next, Vice Admiral Cochrane ordered a disappointed Cockburn to sail to Bermuda with a cargo of tobacco and then meet him in Rhode Island. Baltimore would have to wait.

Cockburn headed down the bay in his ship *Albion* on Wednesday morning, September 7. He had not traveled more than 8 or 10 miles (12.88 or 16 km) when the ship's lookout received the signal to turn back. What did Cochrane want now?

Big news: A British celestial navigator had calculated that an upcoming tidal pattern meant the British should stay in the bay. A new moon would bring higher than normal tides and strong tidal currents, creating dangerous conditions at the mouth of the bay. The ships should wait a week or two before sailing on. But delay could mean opportunity. Cochrane still had Baltimore on his mind. The high tides would allow the large ships to get nearer the city. Also, new intelligence had just arrived from a British captain who had done recent reconnaissance near Fort McHenry. He reported that a brand-new American frigate, the *Java*, was sitting in Baltimore's harbor along with two other war sloops. Copies of recent newspapers indicated the city was in general alarm at the prospect of an attack. So, with time on his hands and confidence that they could once again find the enemy in a weakened state, Cochrane had changed his mind. Instead of Rhode Island, Baltimore would be the next target.

As he peered toward the horizon aboard his packet vessel, Frank Key was beginning to wonder if he and John Skinner, the prisoners' agent, would even find the British fleet. At around noon Wednesday, September 7, they spotted the *Tonnant's* towering sails at the mouth of the Potomac moving up the Chesapeake. A sailor on the *Tonnant* recorded in the ship's log that at 2:10 p.m. the flagship anchored and brought two passengers on board.

Vice Admiral Cochrane welcomed them, and soon the Great Bandit appeared. Skinner had met with Cockburn before and had cultivated a good relationship with him, or so he thought.

Admiral Cochrane's ship, the *Tonnant*, was built to be an imposing warship with three gun decks holding 80 cannons. Most ships of the line carried between 60 and 120 cannons.

British Major General Robert Ross was popular with his troops.

He could tell the Bandit had a lot on his mind. Key mentioned their mission to free Beanes and it "was received so coldly, that [Key] feared it would fail." Cockburn described Beanes in harsh terms and the Americans' hope dimmed.

The British officers invited the Americans to join them for the midafternoon meal, a typical courtesy of the time since they were on an official mission for the American government. Skinner sat to the right of Vice Admiral Cochrane; Key sat to the right of Rear Admiral Edward Codrington. Neither Skinner nor Key immediately noticed the reserved officer seated on Skinner's right, General Robert Ross, the person who they later learned would decide prisoner Beanes' fate. The dinner started out with small talk and then one of the officers made a negative remark about an American. Skinner held his tongue at first, but finally couldn't take it. He shot back a defense of the American and a heated exchange began. Soon General Ross invited Skinner to discuss the Beanes business privately in Cochrane's cabin, leaving Key to diplomatically dine with the others.

Since Ross's Marines had captured Beanes, Ross, as the commanding officer, would decide Beanes' fate. He had ignored a request by letter once but now the requestors were in front of him. Ross quickly read the letters from the British prisoners that Key and Skinner had delivered. They spoke of excellent treatment given to them by their American captors.

Ross said, "Mr. Skinner, it gives me great pleasure to acknowledge the kindness with which our officers left at Bladensburg have been treated. I wish you therefore to say to him [Beanes] and to the friends of Dr. Beanes that, on that account, and not from any opinion of his own merit, he shall be released to return with you."

British Major General Robert Ross was a forty-seven-year-old, blue-eyed Irishman. He had grown up in the same region of Northern Ireland that Sam Smith's family had emigrated from. He had been personally selected by one of Britain's most famous military leaders, the Duke of Wellington, to lead an expedition on America's East Coast. A general for only a year, he had already proven himself many times in battle after battle across Europe. Brave and daring, he was known as a strict disciplinarian but also considered straightforward, fair, even easygoing. He stayed by his troops in battle and earned their undying loyalty. Seriously wounded in the neck in a battle in southern France earlier that year, he had accepted the American command with some hesitation. He had arrived in American waters only the previous month.

Ross would later tell Key that Beanes "deserved much more punishment than he had received; but that he felt himself bound to make a return for the kindness which [had] been shown to his wounded officers."

Just like that Ross had decided to free Beanes. No legal arguments or pleas for sympathy were needed from lawyer Key, though according to his later account, he made sure to sing the praises of Beanes' good character. Recalling the event years later, Skinner

How do we know what happened during Key's meeting with the British officers?

After a September 2 letter to his mother stating he was going to find the British officers, Key never wrote down his actions beyond that point. Details of the meeting come from two main sources: John Skinner's memories written down in 1849; and a long letter that Frank's brother-in-law, Roger B. Taney (future Chief Justice of the Supreme Court), wrote in 1856 stating that Frank told him the details shortly after the Battle of Baltimore. British ship records also provide details regarding when and who met to discuss the release.

Historians who study primary source documents need to analyze the writer's motives. There are two main versions of the story, one giving Skinner a leading role in securing Beanes' release and one emphasizing Key's role. Clearly Skinner, as the prisoner's agent, wanted to take credit for securing the release. Key would want to show that it was his persuasive skills as a lawyer that won Beanes' release. That is, after all, why he was along on the journey.

gave Key no credit for winning Beanes' freedom. According to the accounts, Skinner's negotiation wasn't required either.

Whatever the conversation at the dinner table, Key was clearly not impressed with the conduct of the British. He wrote to his friend John Randolph three weeks later: "Never was a man more disappointed in his expectations than I have been as to the character of British officers. With some exceptions, they appeared to be illiberal [narrowminded, bigoted], ignorant and vulgar, seem filled with a spirit of malignity [spite] against everything American." But he added, "Perhaps, however, I saw them in unfavorable circumstances."

Admiral Cochrane attempted to be a gracious host and apologized that there was no room for Key, Skinner, and Beanes on the flagship. He offered them accommodation on his son Thomas's ship the *Surprise*, where he was sure they would be comfortable. Skinner asked Cochrane whether they could leave to return home the next day. "Ah, Mr. Skinner," the admiral replied, "after discussing so freely as we have done in your presence our purposes and plans, you could hardly expect us to let you go on shore now in advance of us. You will have to remain with us until all is over, when I promise you there shall be no further delay."

Surrounded by a swirl of activity aboard the *Tonnant*, the Americans most likely had caught on to the attack on Baltimore that was in the works. Towing the Americans' sloop, the *Surprise* steered in full sail toward Baltimore. Key had heard plans for the plunder and desolation of Baltimore, and Cochrane had even hinted that the city would be burned. While the purpose of their mission had been successfully fulfilled, Key and Skinner were now under guard with a secret they could not deliver to their countrymen.

CHAPTER

8

NORTH POINT

The fifty-vessel British armada slowly moved up the Chesapeake Bay toward Baltimore, a formidable sight unfamiliar to most Americans.

American Major General Samuel Smith had wisely stationed lookouts along the Chesapeake, who gave regular reports and would send immediate notification if the British armada was sighted. Every day, Major William Barney climbed the 149 steps of the steep spiral staircase to the top of the great wooden dome of the statehouse in Annapolis. He peered through his telescope and scanned the horizon. Day after day his report read, "there is nothing in sight."

But suddenly on September 10, white sails appeared. "Noon, 6 or 7 sail below Plum Point . . . 1:30 p.m. 12 ships in sight . . . 4:00 p.m. 31 ships . . ." They kept coming. By 8:00 p.m. he

The Maryland statehouse in Annapolis is topped by the largest wooden dome in the United States constructed without nails. The tallest building in the city, it was the perfect spot for a lookout.

British Midshipman Barrett of the frigate *Hebrus* wrote: "As we ascended the bay, alarm guns were fired in all directions; thus, testifying the terror which the inhabitants of the surrounding country felt at the approach of the British arms . . . As we passed the picturesque town of Annapolis . . . we could plainly perceive the inhabitants flying in all directions. This was a mournful picture of the times, and should never be forgotten by America when some ruthless politician or party would again wish to plunge their country into war."

counted fifty total. The British were on the move. Throughout the day, Barney had been sending express riders directly to Sam Smith with the most up-to-date intelligence.

Smith was fairly certain that a British land attack would begin at North Point, the tip of a peninsula formed where the Back and Patapsco Rivers met and flowed into the Chesapeake Bay. The location was 15 miles (24.1 km) by road to Baltimore, 10 (16 km) by sea, and safely out of range of Fort McHenry's guns. Fortunately, a lookout had been posted at North Point for the past several years to track enemy ship movement. The Ridgely House, a brick building with a tall cupola, sat on the point overlooking the broad expanse of the Chesapeake. It was perfectly situated to allow the lookout to observe activity approaching Baltimore.

On Sunday morning, September 11, shortly after noon, a dreaded white flag appeared over the Ridgely House cupola, signaling that British ships were coming up the bay toward Baltimore. Lookouts on Federal Hill in the city were always watching. Federal Hill overlooked Baltimore harbor and served as a flag signal station to notify the city's citizens of ship arrivals. Observing North Point's white flag, the lookouts went into action.

Three cannon booms pierced the tense air, disrupting worship services in progress across the city. At Wilkes Street Methodist Church, the minister gave a quick benediction: "My brethren and friends, the alarm guns have just fired. The British are approaching and, commending you to God and the word of His Grace, I pronounce the benediction, and may the God of battles accompany you." At the Light Street Methodist Church, the Reverend John Gruber took a different approach saying "May the Lord bless King

George, convert him, and take him to heaven, as we want no more of him!" Reverend Kemp at Mary Pickersgill's church, St. Paul's Episcopal, offered a prayer for protection: ". . . on this memorable day, give us grace to receive a continuance of thy protection and of thy favors . . ."

Church bells began ringing and soldiers ran to grab their guns and report for duty. Streets filled with chaos, people moving in all different directions. Some of the wealthier Baltimoreans fled to their country residences; those who had family outside the city went to stay with them. But many, like artist Rembrandt Peale, wanted to protect their property in the city and decided to face the attack and endure whatever came. Peale had just opened a new museum, the very first structure in America constructed specifically to display paintings and natural history specimens. If the British came to ransack the city, he hoped the presence of his family of eight children would dissuade them from damaging his new museum.

Unfortunately, historical evidence doesn't tell us what Thomas Kemp and Mary Pickersgill decided to do. They did not leave a journal or any letters to indicate where they were during the Battle of Baltimore. Most, if not all, of Kemp's workers would have been involved in military efforts. Kemp had extended family near St. Michaels. Maybe he packed up his family and went to take refuge with them. But perhaps he stayed to do whatever he could to guard his shipyard. Pickersgill's family was all in the city. Her household may have answered the call of one newspaper: "The patriotic ladies of the city, have now an opportunity of rendering assistance to their country-men in arms, by sending old linen or muslin, to Mr. Gaichel at the city hospital for the benefit of those who may be wounded."

The secret letter from Cockburn to Cochrane stating that "both Annapolis and Baltimore are to be taken without difficulty from the land side ..." (see arrow).

☆ ☆ ☆

The British officers had done their homework. Admiral George Cockburn had sent men at various times to take depth soundings and gather intelligence. And, just as Smith had predicted, the British decided that the shallow, sandy shore of North Point would be the perfect spot to land their troops. Second Lieutenant George Robert Gleig, the eighteen-year-old Scottish soldier, wrote "It was determined to land here, rather than ascend the river, because the Patapsco, though broad, is far from deep. It is, in fact, too shallow to admit a line of battle ship."

As part of his reconnaissance efforts, Cockburn sent a secret letter to his superior Vice Admiral Cochrane in July 1814. "Baltimore is . . . extremely difficult of access to us from sea, we cannot in ships drawing above sixteen feet, approach nearer even to the mouth of the Patapsco than 7 or 8 miles and Baltimore is situated twelve miles up it, having an extensive population mostly armed, and a fort for its protection about a mile advanced from it on a projecting point where the river is so narrow as to admit of people conversing across it, and this fort I am given to understand is a work which has been completed by French engineers with considerable pains and at much expense, and is therefore of a description only to be regularly approached, and consequently would require time to reduce, which I conceive it will be judged important not to lose in striking our first blow . . ."

The wooded Patapsco Neck peninsula varied in width from a few hundred yards to 2 or 3 miles (3.22 or 4.83 km)—flat, sandy land indented with slow-moving creeks. A few farms surrounded by pastures dotted the area. About 7 miles (11.27 km) from Baltimore stood a Methodist meetinghouse at the narrowest point where the Bear Creek cut in from the Patapsco and the marshy Bread and

Cheese Creek flowed from the Back River. It is here on a half-mile (.8 km) stretch of land between the waterways that Smith planned his first line of defense. To reach Baltimore, the British would be forced through this narrow funnel. It wasn't without risk, though, because there was always the possibility that the British could cut off an American force from retreat and surround them. Under Smith's guidance, the Americans had prepared various obstacles, such as felled trees, at strategic points along the road to Baltimore that would help block the British. If they overcame all of these, Smith planned to take a last stand in the thick walls of the partially built Catholic cathedral of Baltimore.

The fife and drums set a cadence as Stricker's City Brigade marched out around 3:00 p.m. on Sunday. A crowd cheered. Smith had selected his best militia brigade for the task. Mostly men of Baltimore—no doubt among them Pickersgill's neighbors and Kemp's workers, carpenters, sailmakers—some had been at Bladensburg. They were eager to restore their wounded pride from that embarrassing encounter with the British. Their commander, Brigadier General John Stricker, had served under Smith in the past and was a veteran of the Revolutionary War. They reached the Methodist church around 8:00 p.m. and prepared for a long night without tents, sleeping on the bare ground. Despite the breezes coming from the water, the night was warm and the next day promised to be very hot.

A militia company commander named James Piper later described the scene: "Our guns were charged, our ammunition boxes replenished and our matches lighted and our eyes anxiously directed to the eastern hills and the main road leading from North Point, for hours expecting to see the enemy in full force to commence the onslaught."

The scene at North Point would have looked similar to this. Disembarking troops from multiple warships was a long process that took hours. Small boats shuttled the soldiers and supplies to the shore.

British Lieutenant Gleig was also anxious, thinking about what the next day would bring. He wrote in his diary: "There was something in this state of preparation at once solemn and exciting . . . we lay at this time within two miles of the shore . . . around us were moored numerous ships . . . The voices of the sentinels, as they relieved one another on the decks; and the occasional splash of oars, as a solitary boat rowed backwards and forward to the admiral's ship for orders, sounded peculiarly musical in the perfect stillness of a calm night."

The still night Gleig described soon became filled with activity. Beginning at 3:00 a.m. on September 12, British soldiers began boarding small boats and rowing toward shore. These were the troops who would attack Baltimore by land. Each soldier carried three days of provisions and eighty rounds of ammunition. In addition, each could take only one blanket, a spare shirt, and an extra pair of shoes. Orders commanded them to share hairbrushes and other personal articles.

☆ ☆ ☆

The *Madagascar* and a few other gunboats moved to within 250 yards (228.6 m) of the shore, ready to fire should an American force materialize to oppose the landing.

Over several hours, a total of about 4,700 troops disembarked from the many ships in the armada. This included a six-hundred-man naval brigade, every sailor and Royal Marine who could be spared. The Colonial Marines—the black troops—also took their place in the lineup, including Ezekiel Loney, the former slave of Corotoman plantation. Horses pulling six field cannons and two howitzers joined the formation. At 7:00 a.m. the bugles sounded and the first troops started toward Baltimore. Once again, as at Washington, General Ross and Rear Admiral Cockburn, side by side, lead the procession on horseback.

By 8:00 a.m. the front column of troops had traveled almost 4 miles (6.44 km) up the peninsula with no resistance from the Americans, short of the fallen trees.

Ross and Cockburn halted at the Robert Gorsuch farm and ordered the family to make them breakfast. They would enjoy a good meal while waiting for the columns to catch up. The troops at the front had made good time, but the day was warming up and some soldiers were passing out from heat exhaustion. While Ross and Cockburn were eating a country breakfast, their patrols brought in three captured American soldiers. The officers questioned the Americans about their defenses;

Map of

BATTLE OF BALTIMORE

September 12-14

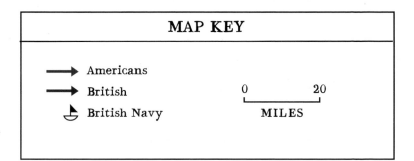

MAP KEY	
→ Americans	
→ British	0 ———— 20
⚓ British Navy	MILES

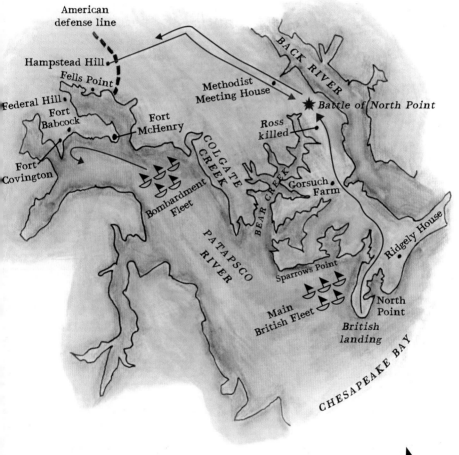

BALTIMORE

American
defense line

Hampstead Hill
Fells Point

Federal Hill
Fort
Babcock
Fort
McHenry

Fort
Covington

Bombardment
Fleet

COLGATE
CREEK

Methodist
Meeting House

BACK RIVER

✳ *Battle of North Point*

Ross
killed

Gorsuch
Farm

BEAR CREEK

Ridgely House

PATAPSCO
RIVER

Sparrows Point

Main
British Fleet

North
Point

British
landing

CHESAPEAKE BAY

N

Ross asked if many of the troops were militia, as they had been in Bladensburg.

"I don't care if it rains militia," Ross replied. He was ready to get rid of anyone in his way. With fresh memories of scared American militia in Bladensburg, he was feeling very confident.

When the officers finally pushed away from the table, Mr. Gorsuch asked if he should prepare a meal for them on their return that evening. Ross reportedly replied, "No. I shall sup in Baltimore tonight—or in hell."

Ross and Cockburn mounted their horses and continued on their way. Ross, especially, was eager to proceed. It was important defensively, however, for the troops to stay in tight formation and not get spread out. The advance soldiers were getting too far ahead of the column. Sudden loud shots ahead startled the commanders. The Americans had made their presence known. Ross decided to ride back and check on his lagging soldiers. As he and his aides turned their horses around, he heard more shots and felt a bullet tear into his right arm and lodge in his chest. In acute pain, he fell off his horse. The horse bolted past the arriving troops. This caught their attention. A running, riderless horse was not a good sign. Cockburn and other shocked officers soon surrounded Ross and immediately sent for a surgeon. Gleig later recalled, "All eyes were turned upon him as we passed, and a sort of involuntary groan ran from rank to rank, from the front to the rear of the column." The surgeon realized it was a grave injury and recommended he be placed on a cart and taken back to the ships. Ross died from his wounds on the way. In his official report afterward, Cockburn described his feelings: ". . . my gallant and highly valued friend, the Major General, received a musket ball through his arm into his breast, which proved fatal to him . . . Our country, sir, has lost one of its best and bravest soldiers . . ."

The forward American defense line had grown restless in anticipation of battle. What was keeping the British troops? Stricker wondered if perhaps the British were going to wait until night and launch a bayonet charge to frighten the militias. He decided to provoke a battle on his terms where he might gain an advantage. He assembled an advance force of about three hundred men, including riflemen, that would march to the enemy.

Neither side was expecting to meet the other where they did. Soon gunfire popped through the hot air. The advance American forces quickly realized they were outnumbered and withdrew back to the main force. Cockburn later reported: "The Americans took to their heels in all directions." But this was only the beginning.

At first, the advance British forces began to pursue the Americans, but they suddenly realized that this was not the main American force. Separated from Cockburn at that moment, Colonel Arthur Brooke, who had taken over for Ross, had to make a decision. "In this situation, [I] had but little time for thought, knowing nothing of the intentions of the General, and without a single person to consult with, I determined on an instant attack."

Around 2:30 he ordered cannon and rocket fire. Stricker was on it and his guns responded. The battle for Baltimore had begun.

The British line advanced, but the Americans opened fire, holding firm. The King's Own, an elite, ancient regiment in the British army, aimed for a gap in the Americans' left flank. But Stricker ordered reinforcements. Brooke ordered a charge and a line of thousands of soldiers advanced through the woods,

Baltimore artist Thomas Ruckle painted *Battle of North Point, Near Baltimore*. He participated in the battle as a corporal in the Fifth Maryland Regiment of the state militia. Years later he created two famous paintings about the battle.

firing as they came. But the discipline of the British military met with a renewed tenacity of the American militias and soldiers. This time the Americans would not run.

The woods soon filled with the dense smoke of muskets and cannons. At times the soldiers couldn't see the opposing side and blindly aimed into the smoke. When the smoke cleared, sometimes they were very close and could look on the faces of their enemies. Lieutenant Gleig wrote, ". . . such was the denseness of the smoke, that it was only when a passing breeze swept away the cloud for a moment, that either force became visible to the other."

Finally, after holding off the British for an hour, the exhausted Americans were relieved when Stricker ordered a retreat of 1 mile (1.6 km) to bring them closer to the main defenses on Hampstead Hill. Unlike at Bladensburg, they managed to maintain a degree of order as they withdrew.

At almost 4:00 p.m. the British were still 7 miles (11.27 km) from Baltimore with several hours of daylight remaining. But Colonel Brooke decided to call a halt. The march would have to continue the following day. The results of the day were 46 British killed, 295 wounded. American casualties totaled 24 dead, 139 wounded, and 50 taken prisoner. The weary British troops prepared to camp at the Methodist meetinghouse at Bread and Cheese Creek.

General Stricker and his forces had done their job. General Smith had ordered them to delay the British as long as possible. Unlike at Bladensburg, they had managed to keep a semblance of order in the face of British fire. The American forces were ready to fight another day.

But from the British point of view, the Americans had retreated.

It had been a "second edition of the Bladensburg Races" as Cockburn's aide called it. They felt well positioned for another day of fighting in the morning.

Meanwhile, on the Patapsco River a few miles away, after the British navy had unloaded the land troops, at first light the sailors began the second part of the pincer movement. They slowly moved upriver toward Fort McHenry. The river was putting their seamanship to the test. They were finding out what the Americans knew well: The Patapsco had a mind of its own. According to midshipman Barrett: "We proceeded without delay under all sail, in company with the frigates, sloops and bombs, etc. to take up a position where we might be enabled to attack the sea defences of Baltimore. Leaving the line-of-battle ships, which, on account of their size, could not proceed any further than North Point, our frigates sailed through the mud for miles. I was in our launch, with the stream and kedge anchors, and cables coiled in her ready to heave the ship off [if they struck ground] . . ." Barrett and his fellow midshipmen were also measuring the water depth and chanting the results: "And a—half—three! By the mark—three!" They frequently grounded on the numerous shoals and he later wrote, "I was literally covered with mud from head to foot in the process." The British knew they were being closely watched by the Americans. Barrett imagined that the Americans were struck with "panic and amazement" at the British ships' progress. He'd been told that though Americans built ships in Baltimore, they sailed downriver with little cargo to ensure the boats wouldn't hit ground. In Annapolis where water was deeper, the Americans would load the ships.

It took great skill to sail a loaded ship upriver as the British were doing.

Admiral Cochrane had shifted his flag from the *Tonnant* to the *Surprise*, communicating his new location on a ship that could get closer to the action. The *Surprise* anchored 5 miles (8.05 km) south of Fort McHenry near the mouth of Bear Creek, while the bomb ships and rocket ship managed to anchor 2.5 miles (4.02 km) off the fort. As a preview of what was to come, the bomb ship *Terror* began firing bombs at the fort to test range and the fort exchanged shots, also testing the range of its cannons.

As Cochrane scanned the activity with his spyglass, he noticed the Americans were busy sinking ships around the fort. This was Sam Smith's last-minute safeguard: additional sunken ships. The Baltimore merchants who owned the ships had initially resisted the idea of sinking perfectly good ships that cost a lot of money in order to save the city. But once the British had appeared at the doorway to the city, they warmed to the idea.

Eighteen years later, Sailing Master Beverly Diggs would give an official account of his activity that day for the court. Owners of destroyed boats had sued the city to get compensated for their lost property. This court testimony offers a look at what occurred. Diggs commanded U.S. Barge No. 7 of the blue squadron of the U.S. Chesapeake Flotilla. At dawn that day he was commanded to take his barge "to the wharves and take such [merchant] vessels as were ballasted and could be easily sunk without regard to whom they might belong and to sink them in the river . . ." Using axes, his crew sank three boats, not making an effort to save any personal articles on board. "It was evident to all that the obstructing of the

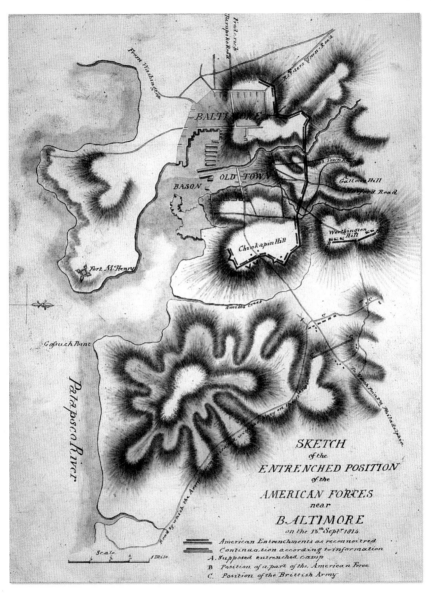

This map was found in the journal of British Rear Admiral Pulteney Malcolm (third in command after Cochrane and Cockburn). It shows British knowledge of American fortifications on September 13, 1814, and the movement of British forces.

channels was the greatest, if not the only real preservation of the city of Baltimore."

At 3:30 p.m. Cochrane, feeling confident and, not having heard of Ross's demise, sent him a note saying that the full bombardment would begin at daylight tomorrow. Four hours later, he learned the news of Ross's death. His immediate concern became to communicate to Colonel Brooke the importance of his plan to destroy Baltimore. Cochrane had recently received a letter from the British commander in Canada with the news that American troops had looted and burned the Ontario village of St. Davids. He had asked Cochrane to serve retribution for this act. Cochrane had been disappointed that Ross had not delivered more damage to Washington and wanted to make sure that Brooke offered no leniency to Baltimore. He promised the bombardment would begin at daylight.

At 12:30 a.m. Brooke responded that "your fire I should think on the town would be of infinite service to us," and assured Cochrane that the army would be on the move again in the morning "to work our destruction."

As he surveyed the activity of the day from his command post on Hampstead Hill, American General Samuel Smith knew that the following day would probably determine Baltimore's fate. He kept busy giving orders and assessing the changing situation. He had to consider the possibility that the British could overpower his troops. What then? The valuable shipbuilding industry, including Kemp's shipyard, could not fall into British hands. The U.S.S. *Java*, a new, almost-completed forty-four-gun frigate that was constructed at Fells Point for the navy, sat as a juicy prize. Kemp's shipyard had furnished the masts and spars for it. As a precaution, one of the ropewalks was set afire so it would not benefit the British should they seize it.

Smith was more concerned with the eastern front and the British troops on land than the ships bearing down on Fort McHenry. He had every confidence in Major Armistead at the fort. At 4:30 p.m., Major Armistead had written his final assessment to Smith. "I have not a doubt but that an assault will be made this night upon the Fort."

The *Baltimore Telegraph* newspaper had given citizens instructions on handling incoming bombs: "We should recommend to every housekeeper to have a servant ready with buckets of water to extinguish the flames." And that night, the Committee of Vigilance and Safety ordered all lights in the city put out in case the British gunners decided to fire on the city instead of the fort. Without lights, the target would be difficult to see.

CHAPTER

9

ROCKETS' RED GLARE

At the crack of dawn on September 13, the five British bomb ships, *Volcano, Meteor, Terror, Devastation,* and *Aetna,* and the rocket ship *Erebus* moved into place just out of range of Fort McHenry's cannons, slightly less than 2 miles (3.22 km) away. The logbook of the HMS *Erebus* reports "at 5:45 a.m. lifted anchor and made sail for the enemy fort. At 7:00 a.m. observed the bombs commence bombarding the fort, fired rockets at the fort, found them fall short, moved nearer shore . . ."

The bomb and rocket ships weren't beautiful to look at like the frigates and ships of the line. But their firepower was terrifying. The 102-foot- (31.3 m) long *Aetna* was armed with two main guns, and 10- and 13-inch (25.4 and 33.02 cm) mortars that fired cannonballs weighing over 200 pounds (90.72 kg) and able to travel 2.5 miles (4.02 km). The *Volcano* held a different type of bomb called a carcass, a hollow shell filled with a highly flammable concoction of pitch, powder, sulfur, and saltpeter, designed to set a city on fire.

The force of each gun firing caused its boat to buck and pitch in the waves. The *Niles Weekly Register* reported: "The enemy bomb vessels 'we are told' are wrecked by their own fire, at every discharge they were forced two feet into the water by the force of it."

The *Erebus's* rockets made a lot of whistling noise but were not accurate and usually missed their targets. The British rockets were often regarded as no more than expensive fireworks. A

H.	K.	F.	Courses.	Winds.	No. of Signals.	Remarks, &c. H. M. S. *Erebus* Monday Septr 12th 1814

Course.	Distance.	Latitude in.	Longitude in.		Bearings and Distance.

H.	K.	F.	Courses.	Winds.	No. of Signals.	Remarks, &c. H. M. S. *Erebus* Tuesday 13th Septr 1814

Course.	Distance.	Latitude in.	Longitude in.		Bearings and Distance.

Sailors on duty kept meticulous records of every action of a ship. The logbook for the HMS *Erebus*, the only rocket ship, indicates that firing at Fort McHenry started at 7:00 a.m.

Frenchman named Louis Simond described them as "made like common rockets [fireworks], only of an enormous size. The cylinder, or case of iron, contains 20 or 30 pounds of powder, rammed hard, and the [front] loaded with balls." The rocket was attached to a 20- or 25-foot- (6.1 or 7.62 m) long pole. "The pole is carried away by the rocket, and keeps in its proper direction like the feather of an arrow. But when the wind blows strong with it, or sidewise, the pole or tail is apt to steer the wrong course, and the rockets go right only against the wind or with no wind."

Congreve rockets were developed by William Congreve in 1804 and were new weapons to the Americans. Designed to ignite fires, they proved ineffective against fortified structures like forts.

The three hundred gunners at Fort McHenry were trying everything they could to get more range from their sixty cannons. They tried several positions to alter elevation of the shot. And they tried putting more powder in to increase power, a dangerous move since the barrels could only withstand so much force. At some point, they were just wasting ammunition if they couldn't hit the British. But the alternative was to become sitting ducks.

Frustrated, Major Armistead ordered a cease-fire. For now, until the British got overconfident and moved closer, they would

Congreve rockets were used at the battles of Bladensburg and Baltimore. Smaller ones fired from portable tripods and larger ones from HMS *Erebus*.

wait. A soldier from one of the units, the Artillery Fencibles, wrote later that they felt "like pigeons tied by the legs to be shot at." The range of the fort's guns was 1.5 miles (2.41 km), shorter than the British range. Armistead knew this. He had asked the secretary of war for larger guns months earlier but had been turned down. The French guns, on loan, had been deemed sufficient. If Fort McHenry's guns failed for any reason, though, a thousand troops waited in the dry moat around the fort to rush to the defense.

After several hours of bombing, the fort was holding strong. Vice Admiral Cochrane began getting irritated at the lack of progress. After all, he had five of the eight bomb ships in the entire Royal Navy. The *Terror*, the most advanced of them, had only arrived in the Chesapeake a few days earlier. It was just over a year old. With its crew of sixty-seven and its Royal Marine artillery of twelve, it could fire forty-five to fifty bombs an hour—a lot of firepower. If they could stay out of range of the fort's guns, they should be able to do serious damage and take the fort. He had been assured that no American forts in this area could withstand the bombs. He would give it a few more hours, but doubt was starting to creep in.

Cochrane examined the American defenses after bombardment began. The British first had to get past the fort's guns, then through the masts of the sunken ships in the channel and the chains stretching across it, then past the eleven barges. Quite the obstacle course. Smith's defenses, including the three barges contributed by Kemp's shipyard, were intimidating.

The residents of Baltimore had never experienced such noise before and would likely not forget it as long as they lived. The *Niles' Weekly Register* reported that "Four or five bombs were frequently in the air at a time, and, making a double explosion, with the noise of the foolish rockets and the firings of the fort, Lazaretto and our barges, created a horrible clatter." One Baltimore resident wrote to his wife, "The firing at the fort has just commenced. Don't wonder if my writing looks as if my hand trembles, for the house begins to shake."

Around 2:00 p.m., a bomb blast shook Fort McHenry. It was a direct hit on one of the fort's guns, killing two soldiers and causing a sudden burst of activity. The Americans noticed that three bomb ships eased closer to the fort. This was just the opportunity the American gunners were hoping for. They opened a fierce bombardment on the ships, pounding the *Devastation* and the *Volcano*. American fire damaged the rocket ship *Erebus* badly and it had to be pulled to safety. In no time, the British ships retreated out of range.

A VIEW of the BOMBARDMENT of Fort McH

Observatory under the Command of Admirals Cochrane & Cockbur
thrown from 1500 to 1800 shells in the Night attempted to land by forcin

References.
A. *Fort McHenry*
B. *Lazaretto*
C. *Solomons House*
Admiral Ship Chesk Part
E. *Ferry and Fort*

...*ar Baltimore, by the British fleet, taken from the*
...morning of the 13th of Sep 1813 which lasted 24 hours, &
...up the ferry branch but were repulsed with great loss.

A View of the Bombardment of Fort McHenry. This iconic view of the bombardment depicts the morning of September 13 and was created two years after the battle by J. Bower.

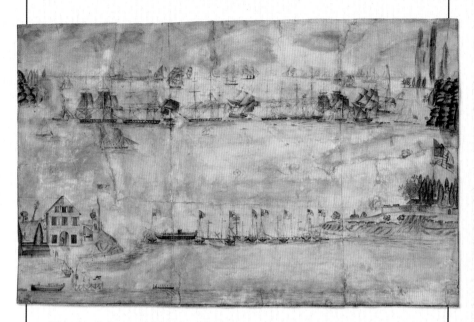

This sketch by an unknown artist is from a perspective behind the American lines somewhere in the Baltimore harbor. It shows the barges, sunken ships, Fort McHenry and its large American flag, and British navy ships in bombardment formation.

Things were not going as Cochrane had hoped. The night before, stunned to hear of Ross's death, he had sent a note to Colonel Brooke with the message to stay strong. Now, he was frustrated and wrote to Cockburn: "My Dear Admiral—it is impossible for the ships to render you any assistance—the town is so far retired within the forts." He was worried about loss of lives and the twenty thousand or so enemy soldiers that his intelligence told him were amassed to the east of Baltimore. Just behind Fort McHenry was a wealthy city tempting him to plunder its riches. But he began to wonder how this battle and the consequences of it might impact his strength for his next attack: New Orleans, an even wealthier city.

My dear Admiral

It is impossible for the Ships to render you any assistance. the Town is so far retired within the forts — It is for Colonel Brooke to consider under such circumstances whether he has force sufficient to defeat so large a number as it is said the enemy has collected, say 20.000 strong more or a less in number, and to take the Town. without this can be done it will be only throwing the men's lives away and prevent us from going upon other services, — at any rate a very considerable loss must ensue and as the enemy is daily gaining strength his loss let it be ever so great cannot be equally felt.

The Enemy has a Better on the

The letter Cochrane sent to Cockburn during the battle: "It is impossible for the ships to render you any assistance-the town is so far retired within the forts . . ." September 13, 1814.

Now in midafternoon, he received a letter from Brooke written at midnight asking for the navy's support of his attack at noon or one. But Cochrane had heard no attack, so something was holding Brooke's troops back.

Brooke and Cockburn's British troops had weathered a miserable night on land, camped in the open, enduring torrential rain. As the new day dawned, they began marching again, ever closer to Baltimore.

Finally, they reached the American defenses. To their surprise, Hampstead Hill rose up before them. Cockburn and Brooke climbed to the second floor of a nearby house owned by Judge Thomas Kell to get a better view of the situation. The enemy was much more entrenched than they had anticipated. An attack would require the troops to charge up the hill with very little cover. They could lose a lot of lives. Cockburn was sure there was a weak area. Brooke went on a scouting mission to gather information, but he could not find a weakness in the American line. He and Cockburn decided that the cover of darkness might be their best plan. The enemy's artillery couldn't see to operate in the darkness and a bayonet charge would scare the Yankee militias. If Cochrane and the navy provided a distraction and drew off some of the troops, it might just work. They sent a note to Cochrane requesting the navy's support of a nighttime operation. Cockburn, as always, hoped to attempt battle.

As commander of the land troops, Colonel Brooke had the final decision. He was more cautious than Ross, who probably would have agreed with the aggressive Cockburn. Brooke was finding it hard to commit to a charge if the navy couldn't help.

He knew his reputation as a leader was on the line. Brooke wrote in his journal: "If I took the place [Hampstead Hill], I should have been the greatest man in England. If I lost, my military character was gone forever." He was unsure what to do and called a meeting of his leaders. Reporting to Cochrane later, he wrote the details of his agonizing decision: "I had made all my arrangements for attacking the enemy at three in the morning, the result was that from the situation I was placed in, they advised I should retire [retreat]. I have therefore ordered the retreat to take place tomorrow morning and hope to be at my destination the day after tomorrow—that is the place we disembarked from."

Meanwhile on the Patapsco, Cochrane had also been getting cold feet and thinking it might be best to abort the mission. But the note from Cockburn and Brooke requesting support of a nighttime attack made him reconsider. Cochrane decided to attempt to support the army. At 9:00 p.m. he directed the bomb ships to stop firing, lulling the enemy into thinking the British had stopped for the night. He decided to stage a diversion and asked Captain Charles Napier to lead an expedition to anchor off the southern peninsula just west of Fort McHenry. This meant Napier's force would need to sneak past the fort's guns and navigate through the sunken ship masts. Their cue to open fire at the fort would be a sudden burst of rockets and bombs at 1:00 a.m. This would draw the attention of the soldiers at Fort McHenry in a different direction and they wouldn't offer support of the land battle.

With oars muffled, twenty small boats carrying several hundred seamen and marines set out in the blackness. Due to poor visibility, eleven got separated from the rest, took a wrong turn, and ended up back with Cochrane. Captain Napier now only had nine boats and 128 men.

Prior to the battle, American General Smith, anticipating a possible British move beyond Fort McHenry, had positioned some excellent junior naval officers and marines at Fort Babcock, a smaller defense just west of McHenry. Sailing Master John Adams Webster at Babcock was napping at 1:00 a.m. when the British bombs suddenly began to fly again. Why start now? Then a brief fiery blue flare arced into the sky, a signal from the Royal Navy to their army that a diversion had begun. Webster's suspicions were raised even more when he thought he heard muffled oars splashing and saw what could be light reflecting off a musket. Could a British force have snuck by Fort McHenry? He quickly ordered his men to their posts and commanded them to fire their guns at the noise. The guns at McHenry joined in and the Americans began two hours of devastating destruction of the British gunboats.

British Captain Napier decided his cover was blown, so he opened fire at both forts with the smaller guns on his boats, and a thunderous exchange ensued. Midshipman Barrett later described the night: "All this night the bombardment continued with unabated vigour; the hissing rockets and the fiery shells glittered in the air, threatening destruction as they fell: whilst to add solemnity to this scene of devastation, the rain fell in torrents—the thunder broke in mighty peals after each successive flash of lightening, that for a moment illuminated the surrounding darkness."

A correspondent for the *Niles' Weekly Register* reported, "The houses in the city were shaken to their foundations; for never, perhaps from the time of the invention of cannon to the present day, were the same number of pieces fired with such rapid succession . . ." That didn't stop the city's residents from crowding rooftops on Federal Hill to watch "the whole awful spectacle of shot and shells and rockets, shooting and bursting through the air," as a reporter for the *Salem Gazette* described the scene.

British Captain Napier's effort had been meant as a diversion to support the army, but there were no sounds of battle from the land. What were the land forces doing? When he saw a flare from Cochrane calling him back, he began the slow return to the bomb ships. Napier's boats were in range of the fort's guns, so he had to cling to the far shore hoping the bomb vessels could keep them occupied. When he got out of range, the firing stopped.

A *Niles' Weekly Register* reporter wrote: "All was for some time still and the silence was awful." The smell of smoke permeated the thick air and the witnesses of the night were exhausted and uneasy. What would the British do next?

CHAPTER

10

MOMENT OF INSPIRATION

At first light early on Wednesday, September 14, the Americans looked down from Hampstead Hill and couldn't believe their eyes. The British had disappeared! The scouts soon verified that the British army was retreating. But Samuel Smith suspected a trap. If he ordered his men to pursue the British, the enemy might attack and take advantage of Americans outside the entrenchments. Word came in that the British navy had turned around and was heading south away from the fort. Was this a good time to pursue the weakened army? What should he do?

Smith took pity on the men and later wrote: "All the troops were however so worn out with . . . being under arms during three days and nights exposed the greater part of the time to very inclement weather that it was found impracticable to do any thing more than pick up a few [enemy] stragglers."

In the British camp, morale was low as opinions about the defeat flew. The lower ranks could only second-guess their commanders. Some blamed Cochrane, others blamed Brooke. A major in the Eighty-Fifth light infantry wrote: "The failure of our attempt upon Baltimore has caused much talk amongst us. Many think that the Navy should, even with the heavy loss they might have sustained, have stormed the Fort—others think the troops should have gone on [despite] the Admiral's advice and [lack] of assistance." Another wrote "It was the universal belief throughout our little army, that had General Ross survived, Baltimore would have been in our possession within two hours of our arrival at the foot of the Hill."

British Midshipman Barrett wrote years later: "As a youngster of fifteen . . . I confess, I thought that with a display of ordinary judgement, perseverance, and decision, upon the occasion, the batteries which defended the entrance of the port might have been graced with the colours of Old England; and the numerous merchant-vessels and shipping within the harbor have been our lawful prizes . . . It was with the batteries bidding us defiance—the weather scowling with a thick drizzling rain upon our proceedings—whilst our hearts and spirits were depressed in the extreme—that we retired down the Patapsco River, with far different sensations from those we experienced on entering it."

Corporal David Brown with the Twenty-First Fusiliers wrote, "I cannot express the discontent and murmuring that every soldier felt when he found they were to retreat though every man knew it was to be a great saving of their lives."

Frank Key and John Skinner spent the night in confusion, not knowing what was happening or who was winning. They heard intense periods of bomb burst and then silence. The British had stopped the bombardment at 4:00 a.m. with occasional bursts afterwards. Key knew that if the British took the fort, they would probably take the city. Baltimore was a much bigger prize than Washington. Aside from the destruction, the psychological blow on top of Washington would severely damage the fledgling nation.

Where were Key and Skinner? Their exact location is not certain. By this point their vessel, the *President*, was tied to the HMS *Surprise*, which moved as close as Colegate Creek, three miles downriver from Fort McHenry during the last day of battle.

Mary Pickersgill's flag would have been visible by spyglass. During much of the battle, their boat was with the bombardment squadron in case they were needed to help negotiate surrender. Prior to the attack, Cochrane had asked the lawyer Key whether there was any person in the fort authorized to surrender. Key later told his brother-in-law that he and Skinner "thought themselves fortunate in being anchored in a position which enabled them to see distinctly the flag of Fort McHenry from the deck of the vessel." Yet, the darkness and pounding rain of the night made it impossible to see which flag flew above the fort.

"You may imagine what a state of anxiety I endured." Key wrote to his friend John Randolph after the battle. He and Skinner took turns peering at the fort through a spyglass, but despite the bomb flashes lighting the darkness, they could not tell who held it. Only the first glimmer of dawn would reveal the answer.

Finally, the heavy smoke from the night's bombardment began drifting away, the storms moved on, the morning mists cleared, and it became light enough to make out the flag flying above the fort. The stars and stripes! The tension of several days instantly melted into great relief. Key had penned several poems in his past, and now couldn't contain his joy. He grabbed a letter from his pocket and began scribbling words on the back. "O, say can you see, by the dawn's early light? What so proudly we hailed at the twilight's last gleaming. Whose broad stripes and bright stars, through the perilous fight, o'er the ramparts we watched were so gallantly streaming. And the rocket's red glare, the bombs bursting in air, gave proof through the night that our flag was still there."

Key would talk only once in public, years later, about his feelings at seeing the Stars and Stripes still flying over Fort McHenry.

The flag that Key saw. Over the years, before the flag came to the Smithsonian
Institution, people cut various pieces off for souvenirs.

O say can you see ~~through~~ by the dawn's early light
What so proudly we hail'd at the twilight's last gleaming,
Whose broad stripes & bright stars through the perilous fight
O'er the ramparts we watch'd, were so gallantly streaming?
    And the rocket's red glare, the bomb bursting in air,
    Gave proof through the night that our flag was still there,
O say does that star-spangled banner yet wave
O'er the land of the free & the home of the brave?

On the shore dimly seen through the mists of the deep,
Where the foe's haughty host in dread silence reposes,
What is that which the breeze, o'er the towering steep,
As it fitfully blows, half conceals, half discloses?
    Now it catches the gleam of the morning's first beam,
    In full glory reflected now shines in the stream,
'Tis the star-spangled banner — O long may it wave
O'er the land of the free & the home of the brave!

And where is that band who so vauntingly swore,
That the havoc of war & the battle's confusion
A home & a Country should leave us no more?
— ~~Their~~
    Their blood has wash'd out their foul footstep's pollution.
No refuge could save the hireling & slave
From the terror of flight or the gloom of the grave,
And the star-spangled banner in triumph doth wave
O'er the land of the free & the home of the brave.

O thus be it ever when freemen shall stand
Between their lov'd home & the war's desolation!
Blest with vict'ry & peace may the heav'n rescued land
Praise the power that hath made & preserv'd us a nation!
    Then conquer we must, when our cause it is just,
    And this be our motto — "In God is our trust,"
And the star-spangled banner in triumph shall wave
O'er the land of the free & the home of the brave. —

Frank Key's original draft of his poem includes four verses. It is now safely preserved at the Maryland Historical Society.

"In that hour of deliverance and joyful triumph, the heart spoke. Does not such a country, and such defenders of their country, deserve a song? With it came an inspiration not to be resisted and if it had been a hanging matter to make a song [I] must have made it."

At 9:00 a.m. British Admiral Alexander Cochrane signaled the bomb and rocket squadron to withdraw. It was over. He could not take the fort. He would need to figure out how to tell this

Which flag did Key see in dawn's early light? Mary had sewn two flags. Some historians suggest that most likely the smaller storm flag was flying during the battle due to the bad weather. Barrett and Munroe's quotes seem to indicate the larger garrison flag was raised after the bombardment had ceased. This would have been consistent with military practice at the time. But other witnesses present at the fort during the bombardment describe seeing bombs and shot piercing the flag during battle, and Mary's daughter, Caroline, wrote years later that Major Armistead had asked her mother to repair damage to the flag after the battle. Perhaps both flags flew over the fort at different times during the bombardment. The smaller flag has never been located. The larger flag, today called "The Star-Spangled Banner," is owned by the American people and is on display in the Smithsonian Institution.

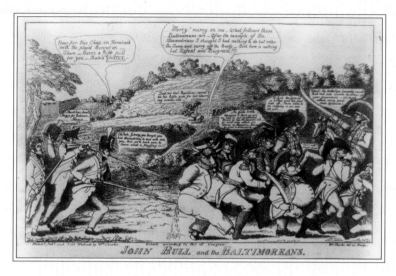

This American political cartoon published in Philadelphia in late 1814 pokes fun at the British failure at Fort McHenry. The Americans at left are prodding John Bull, a popular character symbolizing the English, with Fort McHenry in the background.

☆ ☆

story in his report to his superiors in England. Who would get the blame for this failure? His solution was that he wouldn't call it a failure. He ended up calling it a "demonstration" that had fully accomplished its goals. After all, they had forced the residents to destroy property (sink ships, burn a ropewalk). That was his official position. Privately, he claimed to the Admiralty that the attack on Baltimore was made "contrary to my opinion." He wrote, "I now exceedingly regret my deviation from my original plan." He blamed his lack of numbers—with a few thousand more troops he could have conquered Baltimore. And communication delays had been terrible. Had he received responses quicker, maybe things would have been different.

Cochrane recognized his troops were not happy. He wrote a letter to them that the officers read aloud. It congratulated them for their "decisive victory." "The best proofs of steady and cool bravery are a scrupulous obedience of orders and a strict attention to discipline."

☆ ☆ ☆

Like every morning, at 9:00 a.m., the drums began to pound at Fort McHenry. Private Munroe, an editor at the *Baltimore Patriot* and volunteer at the fort wrote, "At this time our morning gun was fired, the flag hoisted, Yankee Doodle played, and we all appeared in full view of a formidable and mortified [embarrassed] enemy."

British Midshipman Robert Barrett later recalled the sight from his perspective: "As the last vessel spread her canvas [sails] to the wind, the Americans hoisted a most superb and splendid ensign on their battery, and fired at the same time a gun of defiance."

At 10:00 a.m. General Sam Smith scribbled a note to Secretary of War James Monroe. "Sir, I have the honor of informing you, that the enemy, after an unsuccessful attempt both by land and water on this place, appear to be retiring."

☆ ☆ ☆

Key and Skinner could not wait to leave the British and get back to Baltimore with Beanes. The British had no reason to hold them now that the battle was over; however, release would not happen until all the troops were on board, and the fleet was ready to sail. Skinner was doing his job, trying to obtain a list of prisoners. He later reported a brief conversation with the Great Bandit himself, Cockburn, who admitted the attack had failed and offered a different take on the events. "Ah, Mr. Skinner, if it had not been for the sinking of those ships across the channel, with the wind and tide we had in our favor, we should have taken the town."

Late Friday afternoon on the sixteenth, Key and Skinner received word that they were free to go. They sailed past Fort McHenry, carefully navigated through the sunken ships, and eased into Hughes Wharf at Fells Point between 8:00 and 9:00 p.m. People surrounded them, starved for whatever news they could get from the British lines.

Key took a room at the Indian Queen Tavern a few blocks away. Despite his lack of sleep over many days and the exhaustion of his experience, his mind was racing. He sat down and began writing again. He had a song tune in his head, one he had written a verse to before. It was such a popular tune in America that at least eighty-five songs had been published to it. One of these, "Adams and Liberty," was the most popular political song of the day.

Key's tune had originated in England in about 1775 as "To Anacreon in Heaven." It was written by John Stafford Smith, an organist, tenor, and composer from Gloucester, England. The Anacreontic Society was a popular gentleman's club in London named after the sixth-century B.C. Greek poet Anacreon. The society usually met at the Crown and Anchor Tavern in the Strand. The meetings often included a concert by some of the best performers in London. The evening would begin with a concert, followed by supper, and then all sang songs. The first song was always the club's song "To Anacreon in Heaven."

☆ ☆ ☆

Key showed his four-verse poem to Skinner the next morning. Skinner thought it captured the emotion of the night quite well. Eager to find out how his friend Judge Joseph Hopper Nicholson, commander of a volunteer artillery company at Fort McHenry, had fared, Key walked to his house. He shared his poem with Nicholson, who was deeply touched by its words. Two of his volunteers had been killed by an incoming bomb and his sorrow was evident. So impressed was he with the poem, that he asked Key if he could have it printed. Key, anxious to be on his way to check on his family at Frederick, agreed and left to make travel arrangements. Either Skinner or Nicholson took it to the *Baltimore American and Commercial Daily Advertiser*. Fourteen-year-old Samuel Sands, an apprentice, was minding the office. He set the type in the printing press and printed a thousand copies. Nicholson had given it the title "Defence of Fort M'Henry" and had written a brief introduction. Several hundred copies were distributed to the troops at the fort. Though Key's name appeared nowhere on the handbill, word got out. An American private wrote to his brother-in-law, "We have a song composed by Mr. Key of G. Town which was presented to every individual in the fort in a separate sheet . . ."

Key obtained a printed copy before he boarded the mail coach to meet his family in Frederick. Brother-in-law Roger Taney recalled, "We had heard nothing from him . . . and we were becoming uneasy about him, when, to our great joy, he made his appearance at my house, on his way to join his family. He told me that, under the excitement of the time, he had written a song, and handed me a printed copy." Key borrowed a horse and continued the last twenty miles to Terra Rubra, the family estate where his parents, wife, and six children were overjoyed to see him.

News reports from the North arrived in Baltimore on Saturday, September 17, telling of great victories in New York State. The Americans had defeated a British fleet on Lake Champlain and an army at Plattsburgh. They had stopped the British attack from Quebec. Sam Smith ordered the city's guns to fire a salute of celebration. The northern victories had occurred on September 11, the day the British had begun their attack on Baltimore.

Yet, Baltimore remained nervous. Where was the British navy? Would it return to finish the job? "Some say the enemy has gone down the bay—others, that he has received a reinforcement—but the most correct opinion, I believe, is that he still lays round North Point, and is preparing for the fatal blow he means to give this place," wrote a Baltimore resident to his wife who had evacuated town.

But Cochrane had already set his sights on another American city. The British fleet made its way down the bay, anchoring at the mouth of the Patuxent River. Cochrane in the *Tonnant* would head for Halifax and then to New Orleans, the Bandit Cockburn sailed for Bermuda, and a few ships would sail toward the Potomac River, just to keep the Yankees alert.

Key's poem gradually spread in newspapers along the East Coast. New York printed it on September 22; Washington September 26; Richmond and Boston September 28; and then Savannah, Georgia, and Concord, New Hampshire. The local paper in Frederick, Maryland, published it on September 24 and was the first to name the writer. "F.S. Key Esq. formerly of this place." On October 12, 1814, the Holliday Street Theater in Baltimore presented the first public performance of the song with its new name, the "Star-Spangled Banner." It soon was a regular occurrence. "I hear Uncle Key's song is sung every night . . . to a crowded audience and with great applause," wrote one of Key's nieces.

One of the earliest printings of Frank Key's poem set to music, printed in Philadelphia.

Despite victories in Baltimore and New York, the war continued. When would negotiators in Europe deliver peace? On February 5, 1815, the guns of Fort McHenry boomed again to celebrate news from the South, a great victory in New Orleans! Major General Andrew Jackson's army had stopped a British attack by Admiral Cochrane.

The American victories in New York and Baltimore ensured that the American negotiators in Ghent, Belgium, would have a strong case. They had been hard at work and had reached terms of peace at the end of December. But the news took many weeks to reach America because it relied on ships crossing the Atlantic Ocean. Thus, the Battle of New Orleans was fought in January after the treaty had been finalized (though not yet signed), and before the news reached New Orleans. The victory in New Orleans had no bearing on the treaty details.

On February 15, the headline of the *American and Commercial Daily Advertiser* in Baltimore read "Glorious News! Treaty of Peace." The following day, official word of peace reached Washington. President Madison signed the Treaty of Ghent, and the Senate ratified it a day later.

But communication was slow to reach Cochrane. From New Orleans, he sailed for the Chesapeake Bay ready to menace Baltimore in case President Madison rejected the peace treaty. Finally, on March 7, near Georgia where he was to rendezvous with Admiral Cockburn, Cochrane learned that the treaty had been ratified. He turned and set sail toward Great Britain.

The war was officially over. America had secured her independence a second time.

The United States and Great Britain would never go to war against each other again.

This allegory uses symbolism to depict peace. Great Britain and America, symbolized by two women, hold olive branches before an altar. Sailors hold British and American flags and a blank banner. A dove representing peace flies out of a triangle at top center.

☆ ☆ ☆

As for Baltimore, after almost three years of fear and a fierce enemy attack, it was time to celebrate Jackson's victory and peace. The mayor called for February 15 to be a day of celebration with a national salute during the day and a grand illumination from seven to nine in the evening.

Cannons boomed three times throughout the day from Hampstead Hill and Federal Hill, signaling a national salute and using powder captured from the British at North Point!

That evening "every street, lane, and alley blazed with lights." All the street-facing windows in every building were lit with candles and colored lamps. An elegant chandelier hung in front of one home. Throughout the city, elaborate painted transparencies backlit with candles depicted scenes of triumph. A spectacular transparency at Rembrandt Peale's museum showed "peace" as a person and an American eagle grasping an emblem of war in its talons and holding an olive in its beak, which a dove was plucking.

Boys marched down the streets with lighted candles, bells rang, bonfires crackled, and bands played.

The joyous residents of Baltimore banished the darkness of war with light, confident in a bright future to come.

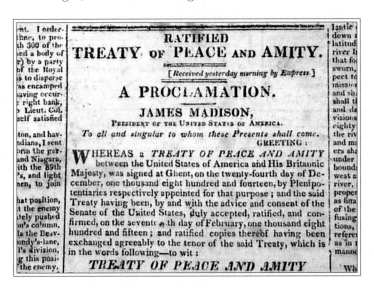

News of peace spread quickly throughout the country. Many cities held illuminations and parades to celebrate.

★ EPILOGUE ★

WHAT HAPPENED TO . . . ?

MARY PICKERSGILL—Pickersgill repaired bomb damage to the flags shortly after the battle. The following year she sewed another flag for the fort. Her daughter, Caroline, eventually married, and her husband moved into the house and began supporting the family. Pickersgill became involved in a cause dear to her, helping widows, and she was elected president of the Impartial Female Humane Society. Years later, Pickersgill helped to found the Aged Women's Home. Such homes to care for elderly single or widowed women were rare at the time. She died at age eighty and neither her obituary nor the description of her in the family bible mention her role in sewing America's most famous flag. She was buried in Loudon Park Cemetery in Baltimore. While most Americans today know the name Betsy Ross, few have ever heard of Mary Pickersgill.

THOMAS KEMP—When the war ended in early 1815, there was no need for more privateers and the shipbuilding boom slowed down. Kemp moved to property on Wade's Point outside St. Michaels and began building a house overlooking the Chesapeake Bay. He spent much time designing it and overseeing its construction, recording the progress in diaries that still exist today. In 1821, his family moved into the house. While he kept active shipbuilding in St. Michaels, his main source of income came from crops grown on his farm, such as apples, tobacco, rye, wheat, and potatoes. In 1824, ten years after the Battle of Baltimore, he died and was buried in a family plot on his property.

MAJOR GENERAL SAMUEL SMITH—About a month after the battle, Smith resigned from the military, ending a forty-four-year military career. His political career continued for another twenty-two years. In 1815, he had the opportunity to join his Senate colleagues in ratifying the peace treaty ending the war with Britain. He was elected to the House of Representatives again, representing the people of Baltimore, and to the Senate again, where he served as president pro tempore a second time. In 1835, the people of Baltimore elected eighty-three-year-old Smith their mayor. At that time, Baltimore was the fastest growing city in America with over one hundred thousand residents. After serving as mayor for three years, he retired and died six months later. His funeral

The first known photograph of Mary's flag, the Star-Spangled Banner, was taken at the Boston Navy Yard in 1873.

procession was the largest Baltimore had ever seen and included all of the nation's top leaders from Washington, including President Martin Van Buren. The guns of Fort McHenry were fired in his honor and his body was buried in Westminster Cemetery in Baltimore.

VICE ADMIRAL SIR ALEXANDER COCHRANE—After his defeat by General Andrew Jackson in New Orleans, Cochrane returned to England. Although many leaders in Britain's military blamed him for the British failures during the War of 1812, he was promoted to full admiral in 1819 and knighted for his service in the war. He died in Paris in 1832.

REAR ADMIRAL SIR GEORGE COCKBURN—Already famous in England as the man who terrorized America and burned Washington, D.C., Cockburn received another assignment in 1815 that would add to his fame. He was hand-picked to escort defeated French emperor Napoleon Bonaparte to exile on a remote island. Eventually, he reached the highest rank in the navy and was elected to Parliament. He also returned to America two decades later as commander of the North American Station and was based in Canada. At his death, a British publication described him as "one of the ablest and most distinguished officers that ever wore the Royal naval uniform."

FRANCIS SCOTT KEY—Key continued to practice law in Washington, D.C., arguing more cases before the U.S. Supreme Court and becoming district attorney of Washington, D.C. He remained active in the American Colonization Society and served as vice president of the American Bible Society for many years. He fathered eleven children. While visiting his daughter in Baltimore in 1843, he died unexpectedly. He is buried in Frederick, Maryland. An American flag flies day and night near his grave.

COLONIAL MARINES—Over two hundred Colonial Marines served in the Chesapeake regiment and fought at both Washington and Baltimore. Four were killed at the Battle of Baltimore. With the end of the war, the British sent them to Bermuda, where they helped build a dockyard for the Royal Navy. After fourteen months, the British discharged them and offered to settle them as farmers on the British island of Trinidad. About four hundred accepted the offer, including some from other regions of the United States. Along with their families, they created villages, many staying with colleagues from their military companies. Ezekiel Loney and his family were among them. They identified as Americans and called themselves "the Merikins."

KEY'S POEM—"The Star-Spangled Banner" poem that Key wrote became a popular patriotic song during Key's lifetime and the unofficial national anthem of the North during the Civil War. By the 1890s, the army and navy were using the song in ceremonies, and in 1917 they made the song their official national anthem of the United States for all military ceremonies. The sports world soon embraced the song and the first documented performance of it at a sporting event took place in 1918 during the first game of the World Series between the Chicago Cubs and Boston Red Sox in Chicago. (By 1942, the song had become a regular feature of baseball games.) In 1931, after almost three decades of attempts by Congress members, President Herbert Hoover signed the law that made it the official national anthem of the United States. The Maryland Historical Society in Baltimore displays the original hand-written copy of Frank Key's poem and features an exhibition about the battle.

THE STAR-SPANGLED BANNER—After the battle, the large flag came into the possession of Fort McHenry commander George Armistead, who wrote his name and the date on two stripes. A family keepsake for more than ninety years, it gradually became recognized as a national treasure and was displayed on various patriotic occasions. Eventually Armistead's grandson, Eben Appleton, appreciated the importance of giving it to the nation

O! SAY CAN YOU SEE, BY
WHAT SO PROUDLY WE
WHOSE BROAD STRIPES
O'ER THE RAMPARTS WI
AND THE ROCKETS' REI
GAVE PROOF THROUGH
O! SAY, DOES THAT STAI
O'ER THE LAND OF THE

The Star-Spangled Banner is preserved in a dimly lit, climate-controlled case to protect

and he loaned it to the Smithsonian Institution in 1907, converting the loan to a gift in 1912. Today, the Smithsonian's National Museum of American History in Washington, D.C., displays Mary's flag, known as the Star-Spangled Banner. After a $10 million conservation project, this gem in the Smithsonian's collection is now maintained in a state-of-the-art case, on display for the millions of people who visit each year.

it for many years to come.

★ PLACES TO VISIT ★

HISTORY COMES ALIVE WHEN YOU VISIT THE PLACES where it happened and use your imagination to travel back in time. Today, you can see many of the sites mentioned in this story. You can almost hear the incoming bombs and rockets at Fort McHenry and feel the force of their blasts.

- Fort McHenry, maintained and interpreted by the National Park Service, still sits guarding the entrance to Baltimore's harbor. A visitor center tells the story of the battle. On days when it is not too windy, you can help rangers raise a giant Star-Spangled Banner on the flagpole.
- Mary Pickersgill's house is open to visitors and preserved as the Star-Spangled Banner Flag House and Museum. You can see the original copy of the receipt for the flag and step into the parlor where she conducted business.
- Fells Point remains a lively neighborhood of historic homes at the water's edge. Although the shipyards are long gone, the area's cobblestone streets and narrow homes still give a sense of life during Kemp's time.
- The Old North Point Road winds through industrial, residential, and rural landscapes. You can follow the road and read interpretive markers that explain the Battle of Baltimore. A few cannons still guard Hampstead Hill, now part of Patterson Park.
- The *Pride of Baltimore II*, a reproduction of Kemp's privateer *Chasseur*, is docked in Baltimore. In warmer months of the year, you can explore the ship or go for a cruise. The tall ship *Lynx* is another reconstruction of a Thomas Kemp ship. It sails to various ports during the summer months.

- The house that Thomas Kemp built at Wade's Point near St. Michaels on the Eastern Shore is now an inn, open to visitors. You can stay there and see the beauty of the Chesapeake Bay. Kemp is buried on the property.
- A boat trip out to Tangier Island offers a good way to experience the Chesapeake Bay. Although the site of Fort Albion no longer exists, you can imagine life on the small island during the war.
- Various monuments around Baltimore commemorate the battle. A statue of Sam Smith sits on top of Federal Hill overlooking the harbor.

Visitors to Fort McHenry help take down the Star-Spangled Banner.

✴ TIMELINE ✴

SELECTED WAR OF 1812 EVENTS

JUNE 1, 1812—President Madison declares war on Britain; Senate votes nineteen to thirteen for war.

JUNE 18—Conflict formally begins.

JULY 12—First seven Baltimore privateers depart.

DECEMBER 12—Thomas Kemp launches the *Chasseur.*

DECEMBER 26—British declare a blockade of the Chesapeake Bay.

MARCH 1813—Rear Admiral Cockburn arrives in the Chesapeake Bay.

JULY—Military officials order two flags from Mary Pickersgill.

AUGUST 19—Flags are delivered to Fort McHenry.

APRIL 2, 1814—Admiral Cochrane issues his proclamation to the enslaved community.

APRIL 14, 1814—British reoccupy Tangier Island.

MAY 30—Colonial Marines' first engagement.

AUGUST 14—Cochrane and Cockburn rendezvous in the Chesapeake.

AUGUST 24—Battle of Bladensburg.

AUGUST 24—British burn Washington, D.C.

AUGUST 25—Committee of Vigilance and Safety is formed and Major General Samuel Smith is appointed officer in charge of all troops.

AUGUST 28—British capture Dr. Beanes.

SEPTEMBER 7—Frank Key and John Skinner meet with Vice Admiral Cochrane.

SEPTEMBER 11—British armada anchors off North Point.

SEPTEMBER 12—British troops disembark at North Point; Battle of North Point.

SEPTEMBER 13—British advance toward Hampstead Hill; bombardment of Fort McHenry begins.

SEPTEMBER 14—British small force attack on Fort McHenry is repulsed; bombardment ends; land forces begin retreat.

SEPTEMBER 15—British reembark.

SEPTEMBER 16—Key and Skinner are released; Key writes poem.

SEPTEMBER 17—Key's poem is published.

DECEMBER 24—Treaty of Ghent is agreed to in Belgium.

JANUARY 8, 1815—American troops win the Battle of New Orleans.

FEBRUARY 14—News of peace of Ghent reaches Washington, D.C.

FEBRUARY 15—Baltimore holds a grand illumination to celebrate peace.

FEBRUARY 16—Congress ratifies the Treaty of Ghent, ending the war.

⋆ GLOSSARY ⋆

admiral—A senior commander in the British navy; vice admiral was normally in charge of a military action and commanded the lead ships; rear admiral was a more junior officer.

apprentice—A young person who works for a skilled craftsman to learn a trade, often for a specified time period; may or may not involve a legal contract.

armada—A fleet of warships.

brig—Two-masted vessel, square-rigged on both masts.

celestial navigator—A person who helped the navy's leaders make navigation decisions based on gathering measurements from the positions of celestial bodies such as the sun, the moon, and planets in the sky in relation to the visible horizon. The navigator also provided information about tides.

Chesapeake Flotilla—A collection of gunboats and barges assembled by the United States to stall British attacks in the bay. The men of the flotilla served on land during the battles of Washington and Baltimore.

Congreve rocket—Self-propelled projectile invented by William Congreve, consisting of a cylinder filled with black powder, capped with a warhead and strapped to a long wooden staff to help provide stability during flight; travels up to two miles, launched from ships or on land.

Eastern Shore—Region in Maryland and Virginia east of the Chesapeake Bay.

flag vessel—An unarmed boat identified with a flag of truce intended for official military or government business between enemies.

flagship—The ship carrying the admiral, the top commander.

frigate—Built for speed and maneuverability, a class down from ship of the line. Frigates held from thirty-six to fifty mounted cannons.

fusiliers—Members of a British army infantry regiment.

Great Britain—In 1814, the United Kingdom of Great Britain and Ireland included the countries of England, Scotland, Wales, and Ireland.

howitzer—A short-barreled cannon.

indentured servant—A young person who signed a contract of usually four to seven years with a skilled person to learn a craft; the craftsman was often obligated to provide meals, lodging, and education.

militia—A volunteer military force of ordinary citizens to provide defense and law enforcement in times of emergency.

packet vessel—Small boats designed for domestic mail and passenger and freight transportation.

schooner—A sailing vessel with two or more masts, used for American shipping and fishing, a favorite with privateers because of its design for speed; built all along the Atlantic coast.

scow—A flat-bottomed vessel such as a barge, rowboat, or sailboat.

ships of the line (also called line of battle ship)—A type of naval warship constructed between the seventeenth and nineteenth centuries to take part in a naval tactic known as a line of battle, in which two columns of opposing warships would maneuver to bring the greatest gun power against the enemy. Ships of the line normally carried 74 guns on three decks, but the number of guns could vary from 60 to 120; the Americans had no ships of the line afloat or any ship to match the British navy's firing power until 1815.

sloop—A sailing vessel with a single mast and a fore-and-aft rig.

sloop of war—A small sailing warship carrying fewer than twenty guns.

spars—A wooden pole used to support rigging and sails.

topsail—The second sail up a mast, counting from the bottom.

transparency—A festive decoration of scenes or inscriptions painted on a see-through substance, paper, or lightweight cloth like silk or linen, and then placed in front of brilliant lights.

transports—Ships used to carry soldiers and supplies.

troops—A large number of soldiers.

victualler—A supply ship in the Royal Navy carrying food items.

★ NOTES ★

CHAPTER 1: A Sitting Duck

1   "There is not . . .": *Niles' Weekly Register*, December 24, 1814.
     A September report from a London newspaper was printed in
     December, anticipating that early news of an American victory in
     Baltimore was erroneous.

CHAPTER 2: A Suitable Ensign—1813

11   "the art and mystery . . .": Indenture of Grace Wisher to Mary
     Pickersgill, courtesy of the Star-Spangled Banner Flag House and
     Museum.

12   "The Military Gentlemen . . .": *Baltimore American and Commercial Daily
     Advertiser*, July 30, 1807.

17   "We, Sir, are ready . . .": Vogel, 313.

21   "The flag being . . .": Taylor, 41. The original quote said Claggett's
     brewery, but historians confirm that Carolyn forgot that at the time
     the brewery was owned by George L. Brown and only later owned by
     the Claggetts.

CHAPTER 3: American Prizes

26   "a horde of . . .": Paine, 2.

32   "she was indeed . . .": Scharf, 373.

36   "doth voluntarily, and of . . .": Indenture of Thomas Jones to
     Thomas Kemp. Kemp papers, Maryland Historical Society.

CHAPTER 4: The Great Bandit

39   "I have no hesitation . . .": Vogel, 24.

40   "There breathes not in . . .": Ibid., 4.

40   "This Cockburn is . . .": Quick, 53.

42   "The coast of America . . .": Adkins, 406.

42   "Hot, damp, dark . . .": Lord, 41.

43   "Go on, my boys . . .": Vogel, 26.

43   "every man's house . . .": Niemeyer, 74.

48   "it is hateful . . .": George, "Chastising Jonathan."

★ ★ ★ ★ ★ ★ ★ ★ ★ ★ ★ ★

48   "Cockburn's confidence in . . .": Vogel, 22.

48   "It is almost impossible . . .": Quick, 29.

48   "As grand and imposing . . .": Adkins, 406.

49   "battalion of seven hundred . . .": Ibid., 406.

51   "find and get possession . . .": Smith, 99.

52   "naturally neither very . . .": Ibid., 104.

52   "are getting on . . .": Ibid., 104.

52   "new . . . Black Corps . . .": Ibid., 105.

54   "The lieutenant . . . went . . .": Ball, 479.

54   "the Colonial Marines . . .": Smith, 106.

54   "I thought then . . .": Ball, 468.

56   Taylor, Alan, 235–236. Ezekiel Loney's story. What little is known
     of the slaves who escaped to the British is found in the records of a
     postwar commission established to compensate masters for their losses.

57   "Your masters come . . .": Ibid., 266.

CHAPTER 5: Under a Flag of Truce

63   "addressed the court . . .": Leepson, 23.

63   "first-rate legal mind." Ibid., 27.

63   "His quickness, his address . . .": Ibid., 27.

63   "a citizen of . . .": Ibid., 54.

63   "taken from his . . .": Lord, 241.

63   "any open letters . . . warfare": Ibid., 242.

64   "I am going . . .": George, *Terror*, 24.

CHAPTER 6: A Plan of Action

68   "My friends I . . .": DeSimone and Dudley, 10.

75   "They are throwing . . .": Lord, 235.

CHAPTER 7: No Love for Americans

79   "The worst enemy . . .": Pancake, 119.

80   "As soon as . . .": Lord, 222.

80   "If the reinforcements . . .": Vogel, 259.

81   "As this town . . .": Ibid., 259.

81   "corrupt and depraved . . .": Lord, 43.

82   "the burning desire . . .": Vogel, 106.

82   "all the country . . .": Lord, 43.

82   "You are hereby . . .": Vogel, 58–59.

86   "was received so . . .": Ibid., 271.

87   "Mr. Skinner, it . . .": Pitch, 192.

87   "deserved much more . . .": Vogel, 272.

89   "Never was a man . . .": Pitch, 192.

89   "Ah, Mr. Skinner . . .": Lord, 256.

CHAPTER 8: North Point

91   "there is nothing . . .": Lord, 247.

92   "As we ascended . . .": Barrett, 461–2.

93   "My brethren and . . .": Lord, 251.

94   "May the Lord . . .": Ibid., 252.

94   ". . . on this memorable . . .": DeSimone and Dudley, 138.

94   "The patriotic ladies . . .": Sept. 12, 1814, *American and Commercial Daily Advertiser*.

96   "It was determined . . .": Adkins, 420. How do we know about Lieutenant George Robert Gleig? He wasn't a senior officer, so he didn't keep official records or make major decisions. Later in his life he wrote *A Narrative of the Campaigns of the British Army at Washington and New Orleans, Under Generals Ross, Pakenham, and Lambert, in the Years 1814 and 1815: With Some Account of the Countries Visited* based on a detailed diary he kept while in the military and on letters he had written to his family. In America, the Scot fought in five battles including Bladensburg and Baltimore. Later in his career he was appointed the top chaplain in the British army.

96   "Baltimore is . . . extremely . . .": Niemeyer, 140.

97   "Our guns were . . .": Vogel, 308.

98   "There was something . . .": Adkins, 420–421

102   "I don't care . . ." and "No. I shall sup . . .": Vogel, 293. These two quotes
      by General Ross have been repeated over and over again in history
      books. Historians must determine the source when they use direct quotes.
      In this case, a surgeon with the city brigade reported hearing farmer
      Robert Gorsuch tell this story several days after the battle. A different
      person wrote it in a book many years later. It makes Ross sound arrogant,
      as if he were boasting. But he was not planning to attack Baltimore that
      day. Also, those who knew him said those types of comments would be
      out of character for him. Did he really say them? We may never know for
      sure. Like many notable historians before me, I chose to repeat them but
      with the caution that their source is questionable.

102   Who shot Ross? The Americans initially had no idea they had shot a
      British general. They may have been aiming for officers on horseback,
      but several ranks would be riding. After the battle, several units
      wanted to take credit for it. The argument would last many years and
      no one knows to this day. Legend says two local boys, Daniel Wells,
      age nineteen, and Henry McComas, age eighteen, privates serving
      in Stricker's advance guard, shot Ross. They were killed early in the
      battle of North Point, and became known as the "boy heroes" of the
      War of 1812. Several decades after the battle, Baltimore erected a
      monument in their memory.

102   "All eyes were . . .": Vogel, 298.

102   ". . . my gallant and . . .": *Niles' Weekly Register*, Supplement to
      Volume VII, 161.

103   "The Americans took . . .": Vogel, 298.

103   "In this situation . . .": Ibid., 300.

106   ". . . such was the . . .": Gleig.

107   "second edition of . . .": Lord, 269.

107   "We proceeded without . . .": Adkins, 421–422.

107 "And a half— . . .": Adkins, 421.

108 "to the wharves . . .": Sheads, *H.M. Bomb Ship Terror*, 259.

110 "your fire I . . .": Vogel, 309.

111 "I have not . . .": Lord, 273.

111 "we should recommend . . .": Ibid., 273.

CHAPTER 9: Rockets' Red Glare

113 "at 5:45 a.m. lifted . . .": Lord, 278. HMS *Erebus* logbook, National Archives, United Kingdom. Historian Walter Lord described the workings of the bomb ships this way: "It took enormous force [to fire a mortar gun], and this in turn put enormous strain on the ships every time the mortars were fired. A complicated system of beams and springs tried to cushion the blow, but even so, the jar [jolt] was terrific. It rattled the crew's teeth, shook loose anything not made fast, and sent the whole ship bucking and plunging like a frightened horse. When the mortar was fired, that also lit a fuse in the bombshell itself. With luck, it exploded about the time it landed, scattering fragments far and wide. But not often. While every effort was made to cut the fuse to fit the distance, the shells were wildly erratic and quite likely to burst in mid-air."

113 "The enemy bomb . . .": *Niles' Weekly Register*.

115 "made like common . . .": Adkins, 162.

116 "like pigeons tied . . .": Lord, 279.

117 "Four or five . . .": Vogel, 318.

117 "The firing at . . .": Ibid., 317.

120 "My Dear Admiral . . .": Lord, 280.

123 "If I took . . ." and "I had made . . .": Lord, 286.

124 "All this night . . .": Adkins, 424.

124 "The houses in . . .": *Niles' Weekly Register*, September 24, 1814.

125 "the whole awful . . .": Leepson, 62.

125 "All was for . . .": Vogel, 334.

CHAPTER 10: Moment of Inspiration

127 "All the troops . . .": Vogel, 340.

127 "The failure of . . .": Ibid., 344.

127 "It was the universal . . .": Ibid., 333.

128 "As a youngster . . .": Atkins, 427.

128 "I cannot express . . .": Vogel, 333.

129 "thought themselves fortunate . . .": Ibid., 319.

129 "You may imagine . . .": Ibid., 320.

129 "O, say can . . .": First verse of the U.S. national anthem.

132 "In that hour . . .": Vogel, 341.

133 "I now exceedingly . . .": Ibid., 354.

134 "The best proofs . . .": Ibid., 344.

134 "At this time . . .": Ibid., 339.

134 "As the last . . .": Ibid. (Barrett.)

134 "Sir, I have . . .": Ibid., 343.

134 "Ah, Mr. Skinner . . .": Ibid., 345.

136 "We have a song . . .": Ibid., 352.

136 "We had heard . . .": Ibid., 352.

137 "Some say the . . .": Ibid., 353.

137 "I hear Uncle . . .": Ibid., 377.

139 "Glorious News!" To many people's surprise, after two-and-a-half years
of fighting, the peace treaty restored prewar borders. Had anything
changed? The treaty's tenth article stated that both nations promised to
work toward ending the international slave trade. And Britain promised
to return stolen property: the approximately four thousand enslaved
people who had fled to the British during the war. A year later, however,
Britain decided to pay the United States for their estimated worth:
$1,204,960. So they remained free. The persistence of slavery would
continue until another war would end it for good fifty years later.

141 "every street, lane . . .": *American and Commercial Daily Advertiser*,
February 15, 1815.

EPILOGUE

144 "one of the ablest . . .": Vogel, 394.

✯ BIBLIOGRAPHY ✯

Adkins, Roy and Lesley Adkins. *The War for All the Oceans: From Nelson at the Nile to Napoleon at Waterloo*. New York: Penguin Group, 2006.

Ball, Charles. *Slavery in the United States: A Narrative of the Life and Adventures of Charles Ball, a Black Man . . .* See docsouth.unc/neh/ballslavery/ball.html; accessed February 10, 2017.

Barrett, R. J. 1841 "Naval Recollections of the Late American War, No. 1," *United Services Journal and Naval and Military Magazine*, Part 1, London, April 1841, 455–467.

Bourne, M. Florence. "Thomas Kemp, Shipbuilder, and His Home Wades Point." *Maryland Historical Magazine*, Baltimore, December 1954. Vol. XLIX, #4, 271–289.

Brodine, Charles E., Jr. "War Visits the Chesapeake." *Naval History Magazine*, Vol. 28, Number 5, October 2014.

Cassell, Frank A. *Merchant Congressman in the Young Republic: Samuel Smith of Maryland, 1752–1839*. Madison, WI: University of Wisconsin Press, 1971.

De Simone, Marc and Robert Dudley with Guy Berry. *Sam Smith, Star-Spangled Banner Hero: The Unsung Patriot Who Saved Baltimore and Helped Win the War of 1812*. Self-published, 2014.

Eshelman, Ralph E. *A Travel Guide to The War of 1812 in the Chesapeake: Eighteen Tours in Maryland, Virginia, and the District of Columbia*. Baltimore: Johns Hopkins University Press, 2011.

Eshelman, Ralph E. and Scott S. Sheads. *Chesapeake Legends and Lore from the War of 1812*. Charleston, SC: The History Press, 2013.

Foreman, Amanda. "The British View the War of 1812 Quite Differently Than Americans Do." *Smithsonian*, July 2014.

George, Christopher T. "'Chastising Jonathan': British Views of the War of 1812 in the Chesapeake." See casebook.thewarof1812.info/Articles_files/ChasteningJonathan/dissertation.html accessed August 26, 2016.

———*Terror on the Chesapeake: The War of 1812 on the Bay*. Shippensburg, PA: White Mane Books, 2000.

Gillmer, Thomas C. *Pride of Baltimore: The Story of the Baltimore Clippers*. Camden, ME: International Marine, 1992.

Gleig, G. R. *A Narrative of the Campaigns of the British Army at Washington and New Orleans under Generals Ross, Pakenham, and Lambert, in the years 1814 and 1815: With Some Account of the Countries Visited/By an Officer Who Served in the Expedition*. See catalog.hathitrust.org/ Record/000405661.

Hunt, Gaillard. *As We Were: Life in America 1814*. Stockbridge, MA: Berkshire House Publishers, 1993. Originally published in 1914 as *Life in America One Hundred Years Ago*.

Johnston, Sally and Pat Pilling. *Mary Young Pickersgill Flag Maker of the Star-Spangled Banner*. Bloomington, IN: Author House, 2014.

Leepson, Marc. *What So Proudly We Hailed: Francis Scott Key, A Life*. New York: Palgrave Macmillan, 2014.

Lord, Walter. *The Dawn's Early Light*. New York: W. W. Norton and Co., 1972.

Miller, Marla R. *Betsy Ross and the Making of America*, New York: Henry Holt and Co., 2010.

Niemeyer, Charles Patrick. *War in the Chesapeake: the British Campaigns to Control the Bay, 1813–1814*. Annapolis, MD: Naval Institute Press, 2015.

Paine, Ralph D. *The Old Merchant Marine: A Chronical of American Ships and Sailors*. See www.authorama.com/old-merchant-marine-7.html accessed August 5, 2017.

Pancake, John. *Samuel Smith and the Politics of Business: 1752–1839*. Tuscaloosa, AL: University of Alabama Press, 1972.

Pitch, Anthony. *The Burning of Washington: The British Invasion of 1814*. Annapolis, MD: Naval Institute Press, 1998.

Quick, Stanley L. with Chipp Reid. *Lion in the Bay, The British Invasion of the Chesapeake, 1813–14*. Annapolis, MD: Naval Institute Press, 2015

Scharf, Colonel J. Thomas. *The Chronicles of Baltimore*. Baltimore: Turnbull Bros., 1874.

Sheads, Scott S. *Guardian of the Star-Spangled Banner: Lt. Colonel George Armistead and the Fort McHenry flag*. Baltimore: Toomey Press, 1999.

———"H.M. Bomb Ship *Terror* and the Bombardment of Fort McHenry." *Maryland Historical Magazine*, Fall 2008.

———*The Chesapeake Campaign 1813-15: Middle Ground of the War of 1812*. Oxford, United Kingdom: Osprey Publishing, 2014.

———*The Rockets' Red Glare: The Maritime Defense of Baltimore in 1814*. Centreville, MD: Tidewater Press, 1986.

Smith, Gene Allen. *The Slaves' Gamble: Choosing Sides in the War of 1812*. New York: Palgrave Macmillan, 2013.

Taylor, Alan, *The Internal Enemy: Slavery and War in Virginia, 1772–1832*. New York: W. W. Norton and Company, 2013.

Taylor, Lonn. *The Star-Spangled Banner: The Flag That Inspired the National Anthem*. New York: Harry N. Abrams, 2000.

Vogel, Steve. *Through the Perilous Fight: Six Weeks That Saved the Nation*. New York: Random House, 2013.

Whitehorne, Joseph A. *The Battle of Baltimore 1814*. Baltimore: Nautical and Aviation Publishing Company of America, 1997.

ACKNOWLEDGMENTS

I HAD THE PRIVILEGE OF WORKING AT THE SMITHSONIAN National Museum of American History (NMAH) during the conservation of the Star-Spangled Banner. I will never forget the powerful moment when staff were given special access and my eyes got within one foot of the uncovered threadbare banner. My fine colleagues at NMAH, especially Lonn Taylor, first introduced me to its story.

Special thanks to the staff at the historic sites listed in this book for their dedication to preserving the places where it all happened. I've enjoyed numerous visits to Fort McHenry and other sites associated with this story. Many people have reviewed either chapters or the entire manuscript and deserve my gratitude. Nancy Sebastian Kuch has been a wonderful encourager, wise editor, and adviser. Also thank you to my writing colleagues in the Arlington Creative Nonfiction Writers group, including former member Michael Lasher; and especially Derek Baxter and Mathina Calliope who offered insightful feedback on the entire manuscript. Jessica and Paul Patterson and Petra Blum also contributed comments. Special thanks to Francis O'Neal, librarian at the Maryland Historical Society, and the book buyers at the Arlington, Virginia, Public Library, one of the best libraries in the nation and my local library. I never cease to be amazed at the obscure books I can find in the stacks. The following experts gave of their time to review the manuscript: Amanda Shores Davis, director of the Star-Spangled Banner Flag House and Museum; Scott S. Sheads, ranger-historian, Fort McHenry National Monument and Historic Shrine (retired 2016); Bill Dudley, trustee of the National Maritime Historical Society and former board member of Chesapeake Bay Maritime Museum; and Chris Wilson of the Smithsonian National Museum of American History. My young reviewers gave wonderful feedback early in the process and included Miranda Baxter, Will and Josie Epler, and Benny and Sofia Glassman. Thank you to Abbi Wicklein-Bayne at Fort McHenry and to my cousin Michael Lowery for help with the maps. Finally, my gratitude to the amazing folks at Abrams Books, especially my editor, Howard Reeves. His thoughtful guidance helped to refine and polish the manuscript. And, last but not least, thank you to my agent Alex Slater at Trident Media Group. We connected at just the right time and I value his insight.

✶ IMAGE CREDITS ✶

☆ INDEX ☆

Note: Page numbers in *italics* refer to illustrations.